JACOB'S LADDER.

BEHOLD A LADDER SET UP ON THE EARTH, AND THE TOP OF IT REACHED TO HEAVEN

GENESIS 28:12   JOHN 14:6   JOHN 1:51

Jacob's Ladder

In Ten Sermons

By

J. E. Hartzler

Introduction by

D. H. Bender

Published by
Mennonite Book and Tract Society
Scottdale, Pa.

To My
Father and Mother
To My
Brothers and Sisters
This Volume
is
Most Affectionately
Dedicated

PREFACE

The responsibility connected with the publication of these discourses has never appeared so great until now. Only by His grace and for the extension of His kingdom do I consent to do so.

May I first express my sincere gratitude to the brethren Daniel Kauffman and D. H. Bender who have freely given their service in criticism and suggestions on the work. To Annie Driver (Stenographer) who untiringly gave her service in placing the manuscripts in their final typewritten form. To the many religious authorities to whom it has been my privilege to refer. Also to the many friends who have so kindly assisted and encouraged me by their words and work.

The following discourses are the results of many hours of toil and research for divine light. I fully realize that no man can hold a patent right on truth. All that we have or ever shall have is but a result of God's grace through those before and about us. It is with pleasure that I grant to the reading public the advantage of whatever good they may be able to receive from this publication.

My whole desire is the strengthening of the children of God and the salvation of lost souls. It is only to satisfy this desire that I have complied with the request of friends who have urged the publication of this work.

The plan running through these discourses is peculiarly simple. Without any display of rhetorical or oratorical beauty, and with Jacob's Ladder as a background, I have tried to present the Plan of Salvation in as simple a manner as possible. I have thought it proper to select only a few of the cardinal points used in my preaching, and, as far as possible, avoid details. But with these few alone, it is my sincere hope that many honest seekers for truth may be led into the divine light of the Gospel. Nothing in my own experience has been so great a power in determining my course in life as a few publications of this nature.

I have attempted to use the most simple language and illustrations possible, with the hope that many a tender mind which is just entering upon the sea of research, may early find the all-important truth, the fountain head of truth, the only life-giving and life-satisfying truth—JESUS CHRIST.

Many are the happy recollections which come to mind as I review these discourses. The occasions during the last year when wandering souls were led to the fountain of living water, are more inspiring and soul-satisfying than human tongue can express. It is with the hope of reaching others through the printed page that many who are on the way may receive a brighter experience ; that some wanderer who is on his way into that far country may get a vision of the Son of God ; that some burdened, despondent soul may lift his eyes and get a glimpse of the open heaven. With the hope that on that Great Day some will appear there uncondemned, saved by grace, because of this simple message, do I now send forth this book on its mission of love.—*The Author.*

INTRODUCTION

All successful teachers, preachers and public speakers make use of the illustration, the figure, the simile. It is written of the Great Preacher, "Without a parable spake he not unto them."

Jesus used illustrations and parables taken from life to make the thought clear and send the truth home. When among the rural folk he spoke of the sower that went forth to sow. When among vineyards He spoke of the vine and the branches. When His audience was composed of mechanics, He referred to the builders and the buildings. On the shores of the blue Galilee or the turbulent Jordan He called into play the net, the fish and the fishermen. The miner was confronted by the man that digged in the earth and found the pearl of great price. To the house-wife He made the manner of finding the gem of salvation clear by the illustration of the woman, the broom, the light and the diligent sweeping until the lost piece of silver was recovered. The shepherds of the plains of Judea and Galilee tired not as they listened to the sagacity, tenderness and love with which the Great Shepherd trained, sought and cared for the sheep of the fold. All this to make the way from earth to heaven clear.

A fitting illustration in the hands of a skilled workman is a tool with which he may build a more splendid, more useful, more durable structure for the habitation of the minds and souls of men in this life than any other one in the craft.

It is but fitting, then, that the author of this volume should employ such a striking simile in portraying the Royal Way upon which all men, entering the portals of eternal glory, must travel. The vision of Jacob and the angel-trodden ladder is a very suggestive basis upon which to construct a series of sermons, such as the reader finds in this volume. The figure is a good one. 1. Because the ladder connected the earth and heaven. 2. Heavenly messengers, man's guiding angels, were passing to and fro on the ladder, showing that the way was pure, tried and serviceable. 3. Because Christ—Who is "THE WAY"—was of the earth (human) and of heaven (divine), thus reaching the entire distance man has to travel in going from his non-continuing city here to the New Jerusalem yonder.

The structural outline of this work is logical, rational, applicable and appeals to the mind of the reader with a considerable degree of fascination, so that the completion of the structure is in itself interesting, helpful and edifying. But the strength of this production is found in the clearness, boldness, and faithfulness with which the subjects are treated. The idea of the Plan of Salvation seems to be the leading feature of the teachings and the longing desire for the salvation of lost souls the burden of the heart of the author. The work is built upon the solid foundation of the Word of God. It is braced with logical, convincing, unanswerable argument. It is protected by bold, fearless, convincing denunciations of false teachers and false doctrines. It is garnished by pathetic incidents and heart-searching appeals. It is surrounded and covered by the unsearchable love of the Father and the dying affection of the Son by which this way from sin to salvation; from sorrow to joy; from death to life, was made possible.

No Christian can read these chapters and not be brought nearer to the doctrines of the Bible and nearer to the Author of our salvation and Bishop of our souls. No sinner, with an unbiased mind and heart, can peruse the contents of this book and not realize that God is speaking to him in every appeal, in every invitation contained in its pages. That the minister of the Gospel, the Christian worker in every department of the service of God may find food for the spiritual man and thus be the better equipped to serve the Master, and that sinners may be brought to the Living Way and ascend the Gospel ladder to the abode of Him who said, "I go to prepare a place for you," is our prayer for the sphere of usefulness of this volume—"JACOB'S LADDER."

D. H. BENDER.

CONTENTS

pointment to Divine and Holy Service—Cleanses
from all Unrighteousness—Is Effected by—Surrendered Will—God the Father—Atonement of Christ—
Holy Ghost—His Word—Is Necessary—Is Commanded—For Victory over Sin—For Holiness—For
Eternal Life—Conclusion—No Hope Without—Our
Greatest Privilege.

Introduction—Three Proofs for the Right Way—Is
it God's Plan and Word?—Is it Divine or Human?—
Does it Satisfy the Highest Demands of the Soul
in Life, Death, and Judgment?—False Ways—Unbelief—Infidelity—Scepticism— Universalism—etc.—
Christ is the Way for—He kept the Law—He is
Grace and Truth—He Connects Earth and Heaven—
He Contains—Divinity—God's Plan—Perfection—All
the Christian Graces—He Satisfies the Highest Demands of the Soul—Conclusion—Enter the Royal
Way While it is Open.

Introduction—"All Aboard"—Invitation from God—
Exiled John—You must Accept or Reject—You Decide Your Own Destiny—We Invite You to—The
Royal Way—The Royal Feast—Association of Angels
—Eternal Life—Purity and Holiness—Heaven—Conditions for Coming—Not on "Feeling Like It"—Not
on Being "Good Enough"—Not on "Being Ready"—
Not on "Wanting to"—But Whosoever Will—Believe—Repent—Come—Invitation from God—Christ—
Angels—Friends Gone Before—Conclusion—Accept
the Final Invitation.

"But while he thought on these things, behold the angel of the Lord appeared unto him in a dream, saying, Joseph, thou son of David, fear not to take unto thee Mary thy wife; for that which is conceived in her is of the Holy Ghost. And she shall bring forth a son, and thou shalt call his name JESUS: for he shall save his people from their sins."—Matthew.

"We are somewhat more than ourselves in our sleeps, and the slumber of the body seems to be but the waking of the soul. It is the litigation of sense, but the liberty of reason; and our waking conceptions do not match the fancies of our sleeps."—Browne.

"The vivid powers of the soul are much more active in dreams than at any other time, the perception is clearer, and the sensitive faculties are much more alive when asleep than when awake. We see this verified in the man dying. His eye is usually brighter, his mind clearer, his soul is more free and becomes less selfish, as he passes on and nears the eternal."

THE VISION

"And he dreamed, and behold a ladder set up on the earth, and the top of it reached to heaven; and the angels of God ascending and decending on it."—Gen. 28:12.

No story so pitiful, no wandering so significant, no picture so wonderful and so glorious, as that of Jacob and his vision. The wanderer has gone one day's journey from home. The sun, having set beyond the great sea, was still sending his golden beams of light toward the heavens. One by one the silvery stars appear to drive away the king of day, twilight, darkness and starlight over-take the wanderer, Jacob, fleeing from an angry brother, now forty miles from home on his way to Padanaram, in a strange land, no place to call his home and no friend to share his trials. How weary and lonesome the evening must have been! Weary with the day's journey, he prepares for the night. Failing to find a shelter, he makes his bed on the cold, naked earth, and to make it more comfortable, gathers a few stones for a pillow upon which to rest his weary head. His bed was large. His coverlet included the entire heavens. With all his discouragements it was no doubt the most glorious and satisfying evening of his whole life. No nights in my own experience have I enjoyed so well as those spent on the western wheat-fields with only the earth for a bed and all the starry sky for a coverlet. Many times have I been convinced that "The heavens declare the glory of God and the firmament showeth his handi-work."

While Jacob was lying upon his bed, his experience was not so widely different from that of other men. His mind was on his old home which he had left. No doubt with tears in his eyes he thought of how he had robbed his brother Esau, and how he had deceived his blind father, Isaac. He thought of his blessings and promises. His mind ran into the future, wondering how all this should come to pass. In this weary, troubled condition, he fell into a slumber; but it was not quiet, peaceful sleep. That weary mind was still not at rest. Those life problems were still revolving in his mind. The promises of the future and the coming Savior were yet dark; as he slumbered, he dreamed, but it was not a dream resulting from a disturbed stomach. It was not a delirious vision of fowls and creeping things; not a vision resulting from immoral thoughts and habits, but it was a vision in which God held the motive powers, a vision which should be a blessing to the salvation of many souls to follow. One which would make clear the way from earth to heaven. But as he dreamed,

Behold a Ladder

set up on the earth, and the top of it reached to heaven, and the angels of God were ascending and descending upon it.

Jacob's problem was being solved. The Lord was revealing the plan and work for the Savior; God himself standing above the ladder and speaking in audible tones. How dreadful this vision must have been to

Jacob! "Oh, wretched man that I am, who shall deliver me?" There is but one way, and that is by the way of the ladder. But he failed to take that way. He failed to climb the ladder.

My sympathy has often gone back to Jacob, because he did not in his spirit ascend the ladder with those heavenly beings, those heavenly messengers. What a wonderful experience he could have related the next morning! The problem of the promised Savior might have been solved.

I have often wondered if Jacob had seen several spotted cattle, or if he had seen Rachel at the top of the ladder, whether he would not have gone up, even at the risk of his life. When I look over the human family tonight, I see men and women climbing the ladder of wealth, of honor, of society, of scepticism, unbelief and infidelity, sacrificing their very lives and eternal souls, and never touch the ladder which leads from earth to heaven, from earth to eternal glory, to eternal life: My dear friends, do not accuse old Jacob of his deeds when you are doing no better.

I have often wondered why God set before Jacob such a simple, homely thing as a ladder. Why not a flying machine? Why not a modern elevator? Why not a fiery chariot? Why not some mysterious means of transportation which man could not understand? But I have since concluded that the ladder was used, not for the sake of God, not for the sake of the angels, not for the sake of curiosity; but for the sake of Jacob —for the sake of presenting Jesus Christ, the way from earth to heaven, for the sake of humanity, proving the way as the only way, which must be climbed, and not one of "flowery beds of ease."

Jacob, like all sinners today, failed to climb, because he was unconverted. He was interested in worldly affairs. He was unconscious of his condition, of his dangerous surroundings, of his privilege, of his blessings, and, lastly and most unreasonably of all, he was afraid. Thousands of men and women today stand away and never touch the ladder because of fear. Surely, "The fear of man bringeth a snare."

The position of the ladder proves its purpose. It stood upon the earth and the top of it reached to heaven. It is evident that there is to be a passing from from one place to the other. We know God has power to pass where He desires without a ladder. We know that angels need no ladder as a means of passing from heaven to earth. We must then conclude that the ladder was put up for Jacob, and for every wandering soul from his day to this. There is a longing, a seeking by every human soul to find a way back to God. True enough, human nature in itself does not want God, but there is yet a spark of good desire in every soul. None are so sinful but there is a desire for something better. The passage between earth and heaven was destroyed in the garden of Eden. The bridge has been condemned, another way must be prepared, and God in His mercy has prepared the way.

Some time ago, after preaching on this subject in Minnesota, a certain brother said, "Surely that is a long ladder to climb from earth to heaven." I said,

"It does look long, but remember that with God space does not enter into the distance between earth and heaven. It is a spiritual distance, a spiritual ladder, and space does not enter the question. When Christ said to the Scribe, 'Thou art not far from the Kingdom' (Mark 12:34) He did not use long measure in rods and miles, but spiritual measure in knowledge and understanding."

As the position indicates for whom it was prepared, so the use which was made of it proves what it signifies. Jacob, a wandering soul, lying slumbering at one end of the ladder, God standing above the other end, angels ascending and descending upon it, possibly rejoicing over the fact that man and God would soon be reconciled, that a connection would again be effected between earth and heaven. For this to be accomplished, required a greater sacrifice than the blood of bulls and of goats, more than human sacrifice, more than all the world could furnish. It required the only begotten Son of God. He is all that could possibly bring about a reconciliation, and over Him alone can lost humanity be saved. As the angels of God ascended and descended upon the ladder, which is only a type of what is to follow, I turn seventeen and one-half centuries into the future from Jacob's vision, and find (John 1:51) "Hereafter ye shall see the heavens open, and the angels of God ascending and descending upon the Son of Man." There, my dear friends, you have the secret of Jacob's ladder. There is the ladder in its perfection, the only way from sin-cursed earth to an eternal heaven.

I am convinced that Jacob practically made a

failure of his part of the vision. The key to his failure lies in his unconverted life, his unwillingness to
submit, and as a result of his own condition he failed
to understand fully the vision. What a different
story he could have told in the morning, if he had only
ascended the ladder with the angels and took one
single glance into heaven! How much more he could
have known! How much more such an experience
would have been worth than all his spotted cattle!
How much better he could have explained the vision!
But instead of that he awoke and was afraid. He
favors our so-called professors of today who are willing to make the Lord their God provided they can
choose their own course and the Lord will promise to
go with them and bring them back safely, feed and
clothe them.

But it is now too late; morning has dawned, the
ladder is gone from his view. He may now be lament-
ing his neglect of duty, but all too late! The same
lamentation will be heard from you, wandering souls;
you lie slumbering tonight in the cradle of sin, and at
an unguarded moment you will awake; the ladder
from earth to heaven will be gone, and your awful
cry of "All too late! All too late!" will be heard.
Now notice

God's Purpose

in the vision. God is not a God of secrecy. He delights in making Himself and His ways known to
men. He stood above the ladder and spoke in words
of authority, such as no other dared to utter, "I am
the Lord God of Abraham thy father, and the God of

Isaac." Such a scene and such a voice before the eyes
and ears of Jacob is sufficient to make any sinner tremble. We have no better type of the sinner anywhere;
alone in the dark, cold, friendless world, difficul-
ties, doubts and disappointments at his door. God
has done His part well. He has revealed Himself,
warned Jacob, and set before him a way of escape.
But he is not willing to leave him at that. He has
done more for him. "The land whereon thou liest, to
thee will I give it, and to thy seed, and thy seed shall
be as the dust of the earth, and thou shalt spread
abroad to the West, and to the East, and to the North,
and to the South, and in thee and in thy seed shall all
the families of the earth be blessed." Can man think
of a greater promise? Can any man comprehend the
far-reaching blessing? A promise of land; the land
of Canaan, the best and most productive. Of life; his
seed shall be innumerable, shall spread in all directions and shall remain even today. Of the Messiah;
through whom all the families of the earth shall be
blessed. Even the Savior of the world shall come
through the generations of Jacob. Surely God has
done His part! Proving Himself beyond all doubt,
and promising to the sinner, land, life and salvation.
He promises to accompany him, to guard and guide
him, yet it took Jacob twenty-one years to surrender
his will to God and become really converted. We
have on record at least two nights in which the Lord
wrestled with Jacob, when he finally surrendered with
a crippled thigh. It reminds me much of our experience as Gospel ministers today; we stand night after
night for weeks and months declaring the love of

God; presenting the ladder reaching from earth to heaven; presenting the undeserved promises of God's love; and not only one Jacob lies slumbering on the cold earth at the foot of the ladder, but hundreds of them, trembling with fear because God has been revealed, promises have been presented, and the ladder has been set before them. The way has been made plain, but before they will give up, God must reach out and touch them and disable them by sickness or loss of wealth, of health, or some loved one. But God was not discouraged. He goes on and by and by it is clear that the

LADDER TYPIFIES

the only way from earth to heaven. It was revealed in a way that we must agree that it binds earth to heaven and that we have a part to perform. It is not on "Flowery beds of ease." A ladder, we need not argue, is for climbing. It stood up on the earth and it reached to heaven; not to the herds of Laban, not to earthly wealth, not to earthly glory, but to heaven. It is the only way that every wandering soul may and must travel in order to reach heaven. "All we like sheep have gone astray." We are all wandering; the earth is not our home; we look for a City not made with hands. We look for satisfaction and for rest; even the lowest and most ignorant heathen seeks relief and rest by throwing himself beneath the great Juggernaut Car or the mother by throwing her living child down to the crocodiles. Humanity is seeking its way back to God in many ways; but there is but one way which has been tried and insured, and that is the way which God set before Jacob. "He that climbeth up some other way, the same is a thief and a robber." The ladder is also typical of

THE LAW AND THE GOSPEL

While the law was given by Moses and was without doubt incomplete and very rigid, it was God's purpose to use it fundamentally to point men to God. While it was incomplete, yet it served the purpose of pointing men to Him. The Law and the Gospel not running parallel, we know must meet somewhere, and that meeting place is none other than God. "The Lord stood above it." So in the Law we have one main piece of our ladder. The Law side was not complete. Christ came not to destroy, but to fulfill the Law and He did it with His life and the Gospel.

We have now the Law and the Gospel, which shall be developed in a later sermon, but before leaving it, the Law and the Gospel, or the two sides of this ladder, must be joined by like material, and when complete and erected you have simply the love of God on the Law side, the love of God on the Gospel side, and the love of God joining the two. Hence all becomes one unit simply resolving itself into another form or picture, Jesus Christ. "I am the way, the truth, and the life; no man cometh unto the Father, but by me." Jesus Christ the ladder; the only way from earth to heaven. It is open for the highest and the lowest, the most intelligent and the most ignorant, the richest and the poorest, and above all the most sinful.

In my evangelistic work in the West a young man came forward after the sermon, with tears flowing over his face, to meet me, saying that he desired to start for heaven but feared he was too sinful and too wicked and that God would not accept him. I said, "My friend, the Bible tells us that, 'This is a faithful saying and worthy of all acceptation that Christ Jesus came into the world to save sinners.' 'For the Son of man is come to seek and to save that which was lost.' The way has been especially prepared for sinners, and that includes you." After considerable struggling, he succeeded in reaching the foot of the ladder and taking hold of the first round, faith, he began to climb and tonight is rejoicing on his upward way to heaven.

God and man run unparallel; in Christ they meet. He is the way, upon Him the angels of God ascend and descend. He has fulfilled the Law; He is actually the truth, not a type; He is the beginning and the end of the way to heaven; He reaches the earth in His humanity and His humility; He reaches heaven in His divinity and exaltation; He is really life because He is eternal and divine. There are many ways which seem right, but their ends are eternal death. The end of Christ is life eternal. When I see the heavens open and the angels of God ascending and descending upon the ladder, and God Himself standing at the head; when I see Jacob lying upon the cold earth asleep, I see a true picture of the heavens opening today and the angels of God ascending and descending on the Son of man, the Lord God standing above, the world of sinners lying asleep in sin, not willing to repent, not willing to climb the ladder, not willing to receive the promise, but prefer rather another way, prefer the cold, stony earth, choose rather a way which only seems right, but to their own shame and disgust wake up and open their eyes in death; awake out of sleep and find the ladder gone. They see some of their loved ones across on the other side rejoicing with the angels. All is too late, opportunity is gone and the ladder is gone, no means of escape and heaven is missed; nothing is left but eternal remorse of conscience; nothing but eternal darkness and death, nothing but eternal separation from God and all that is pure and holy, nothing but eternal misery and woe, eternal fire and brimstone. Then will be heard the cry for one more opportunity; for one more hold on the ladder which leads to heaven; for one more hearing at the throne; for one more oportunity of pardon; a cry for a little more comfort, but a voice will come in powerful authority, "Depart ye cursed, I never knew you." Opportunity after opportunity has been granted; time after time has the ladder been placed at your feet; invitation after invitation has been extended to you; pardon after pardon has been offered to you; prayer after prayer has been breathed in your behalf; all these with the pleadings, the tears and blood of Christ you have trampled under your feet. It is now too late. There is nothing for you but eternal hell with the devil and his angels, "Where the worm dieth not and the fire is not quenched." My dear sinners, tonight while the ladder is standing before you, in the name of Jesus and for the sake of your lost soul, make it your way to heaven. Faith in the ladder is the first step. But before I can close, let us notice

The Effect on Jacob

After such a wonderful demonstration of God's power and authority; the heaven open, the angels ascending and descending upon the ladder, the voice of God Himself in powerful tones declaring Himself and convicting sinful Jacob; it is only natural that his first words after awaking should be, "Surely the Lord is in this place; and I knew it not," and he was afraid. "How dreadful is this place! This is none other than the house of God, and this is the gate of heaven," and Jacob felt like every other sinner when God has warned and convinced and set before him the only way of escape. He acknowledges, admits the truth, even trembles under a disturbed mind day and night, yet not willing to repent, and as a result when converted goes limping because of a crippled thigh. How different it would have been with Jacob had he simply repented and taken God's plan instead of his own. He would have avoided twenty-one years of trouble, he would have avoided the night's wrestle with the angel, receiving a crippled thigh. But he took his own course, chose his own way, went against better knowledge, and was unwilling to surrender. He refused the only way to heaven, and I do not wonder that he was afraid, and finally crippled. It is nothing unnatural to see men and women going through life limping because of a crippled thigh. It is nothing unnatural to find men and women so tired of life that they will even seek relief through suicide. But instead of this there is set before you tonight a relief, a way which leads from earth to heaven, a way which is pleasant, one which will satisfy and make you happy, one which is pure, one which results in life, a way which will not always be open but which must be traveled now.

While it is a pitiful sight to see men and women by the thousands losing their souls though the tumbling down of their own ladders, it is more pitiful to see thousands of sinners lying upon the cold earth, slumbering under the influence of Satan's chloroform, while the way of escape is set at their very side. It is a glorious sight to see the heavens open and the angels of God ascending and descending on the Son of man. It is a glorious sight to see the love of God in the Law and the love of God in the Gospel, the love of God joining the two, and as a result of this resolving into one, Jesus Christ, the only way from earth to heaven. Above this way God stands with outstretched arms of mercy inviting sinners to come. The angels as they ascend and descend invite sinners to come. Christ the mediator invites them to come. Nearing the top of the ladder are silver-haired fathers and mothers inviting them to come. Half way up the ladder are strong Christian men and women inviting sinners to come. On the first round, just starting, are young Christians inviting sinners to come. I see sinners tonight who are seriously weighing the matter and are almost persuaded. I see some who are unconcerned. I see some at a distance who only mock and point the finger of scorn. Wandering souls, where are you tonight? My prayer to God is that those of you who are nearing the port may continue to the end, until you have really anchored your soul in the eternal haven; that those of you who have just started may become stronger continually as you advance; that you sinners who are almost persuaded may be not almost but altogether persuaded and set your feet upon the first round, faith, and start on your way heavenward. Will you come tonight?

"Wherefore the law was our schoolmaster to bring us to Christ."—Paul.

"The law of God is what we must do; the gospel is what God will give."—Luther.

"Ignorance of the law excuses no man; not that all men know the law, but because it is an excuse every man will plead, and no man can tell how to confute him." —Selden.

"There is not a book on earth so favorable to the kind, and to all the sublime affections, or so friendly to hatred, persecution, tyranny, injustice and every sort of malevolence as the gospel. It breathes throughout only mercy, benevolence and peace."—Beattie.

THE LAW AND THE GOSPEL

"For the Law was given by Moses; but grace and truth came by Jesus Christ."—John 1:17.

In the sermon last night we noticed the significance of the ladder. One application drawn was that of the Law and the Gospel. To continue this application I invite your attention to the general make-up of the material ladder. For a ladder to be serviceable and satisfactory, to avoid turning and tumbling down or breaking under its weight, two main side pieces or supporters are necessary, running from bottom to top; and to make it more safe the top of the ladder is drawn nearer together while the bottom is spread, making a firm foundation and less chance for tumbling down. Thus throwing the two sides in an unparallel position. Long ago science has plainly proven that parallel lines can never meet, no matter how far they may be extended, while unparallel lines must meet if sufficiently extended. So the two sides of a ladder in this position if extended must meet.

Both sides of a ladder are of like material, from the same forest, very often from the same tree. There no doubt is a difference in the two pieces. They could not possibly be alike in every respect. They may appear alike, but there is a difference in the grain of the wood, in the weight and in the stability; yet taken from the same forest, same wood, passing through the same hands and made for a like purpose. Generally the rounds are hewn from the same forest, from the same material, made by the same company, the mind of the same man and yet used for a different purpose. They are not the supporters, but they join and bind the supporters together. They draw their strength from their supporters, rest upon them, and finally, when the sides and rounds are complete and joined, they are no longer so much wood, so many rounds, but become a complete unit, a ladder.

From these simple truths I draw my application for the Law and Gospel. Both are a development from the same seed,—Love; made by the same company,—the Father and the Son and the Holy Spirit; used for the same purpose,—pointing to God. They differ, however, in several principles, especially in character and time; running unparallel, they meet somewhere; sides joined by numerous rounds drawn from the same forest and finally when complete and joined they stand no longer as so much Law and Gospel but resolve themselves from this elementary condition to a complete whole—the way from earth to heaven.

But allow me to separate this way once more into its elements and notice each part separately. Beginning with one side of the way, one of the two main supporters, one which we must have,

The Law or Old Testament

"The Law was given to Moses; but grace and truth came by Jesus Christ." Generally speaking, in the Law we include the whole of the Old Testament; so I shall speak of it tonight. Moses was not the originator, not the creator, not the mind, not the power of the Law, not the author especially, but the means which God used to transfer to the people and to execute it. The Law was given by Moses, but he gave it only as he received it from God. Law is more than human invention. Law cannot always be placed in literal form. All Law has not yet been discovered, but this much has been revealed to Moses; this much has been given to humanity; this much has been given to serve as one side of this ladder— the way from earth to heaven.

The Law is theocratic in its nature. Its underlying principles recognize God as the ruler of the universe, as well as the Jewish nation. It is a growth from the same seed as the Gospel—passes through the same hands, is of like material, differs, however, in some minor details, but is used for a like purpose—to point men to God. It employs different methods, but fundamentally answers the same purpose. "Wherefore the Law was our schoolmaster to bring us unto Christ, that we might be justified by faith"—Gal. 3:24. It is an outgrowth from the great storehouse of God's love. In fact it is love; it is life in an indirect form. While it is true under the Law that "The soul that sinneth it shall die," I draw a great truth and consolation—that the soul that sinneth not, it shall live. My dear friends, it is life after all, is it not?

We do not claim salvation in the Law alone, because no man save Jesus Christ has ever kept the whole Law. The Law passed a death sentence upon the guilty. The Law connected with faith in the promised Savior was all that could redeem. The

Law is necessary to complete our salvation. In itself it is imperfect. "The Law made nothing perfect, but the bringing in of a better hope did; by the which we might draw nigh unto God." "For what the Law could not do in that it was weak through the flesh, God sending his own Son in the likeness of sinful flesh, condemned sin in the flesh." With all its weakness and incompleteness, the Son of God himself said concerning it, "Think not that I am come to destroy the Law or the prophets; I am not come to destroy but to fulfill"—Matt. 5:17. It was not His work to destroy, to condemn, to blot out, but to fulfill; to fill up the breaches, the greatest of which was death to the guilty, which He filled by His own death. The breach has been literally closed and as a result we have life. Christ did not discard the Law. He respected it and observed it perfectly and was obedient and subject to it.

There were local and temporal things about the Law which were left unobserved. The numerous sacrifices, the temple worship and such like have been cancelled because they were only typical. When the reality came, when the Truth came, the great sacrifice of the Son of God, and the worship in spirit and truth came, those types were put away. When Jesus Christ our High Priest entered the holy of holies once for all, offered his sacrifice, broke down the middle wall of partition, the Law was satisfied and fulfilled; temple worship and animal sacrifice were put away. "The hour cometh, when ye shall neither in this mountain nor yet at Jerusalem, worship the Father.". . . . . "The hour cometh and now is when the true worshippers shall worship the Father in spirit and in truth"—John 4:23. We have no more use for the types except for explaining and supporting their substitutes or realities. For this reason, "He taketh away the first that He may establish the second"—Heb. 10:9.

There are, however, universal principles in the Law which never were, nor ever shall be changed. They have been carried across into the Gospel, and down to the present day and we are subject to them the same as the Jews were and always shall be. "Thou shalt have no other gods before me." Thou shalt not take His name in vain, remember the sabbath day, honor thy father and mother, thou shalt not kill, not commit adultery, not steal, not bear false witness, not covet, and others we are under obligation to obey. "Till heaven and earth pass away one jot or one tittle shall in no wise pass from the law until all be fulfilled."

Make of the Law what you will, we cannot, we dare not throw away its underlying principles. We cannot deny its origin from the love of God. We cannot deny that the Law is love. It is truly, "Our schoolmaster to bring us to Christ." It is Christ, it is life. We cannot deny that it was necessary to point men to God. It is a part of this ladder which leads from earth to heaven. We admit its incompleteness in itself; we admit that there is no salvation in it alone, because man failed to obey it. Something more is necessary, and before Christ's great and final sacrifice, this wanting part was supplied in looking forward with the eye of faith to the promised

Messiah; a looking forward to One who would literally complete the plan, close up the breaches, obey where man disobeyed, give another support to the ladder in its reality, and we have it in

THE GOSPEL OR THE NEW TESTAMENT

"The Law was given by Moses; but grace and truth came by Jesus Christ." Jesus Christ was not merely the Giver, but the Author; it came by Him and from Him. He is the creator and originator of grace, the power and the authority Himself, His mind and His life. He was not only an agent to transfer grace and truth, but He is grace and truth. He is truth, not merely a type, but the reality; the part apparently left out by the law; the part which was supplied by faith; the part typified by the sacrifices; the part needed to complete and fulfill the Law. He is the way because He is the source of both the Law and Gospel. He is the truth because He is real and not typical. He is life because He is love. He is the hidden part of the Law, the love of God, the life through faith. He is the Law, only in a different dress. He was love and Law from the beginning. We may for convenience separate Christ and the Law into elements, but in reality they are one and the same. Christ came to fulfill the law, and in order to do that he must necessarily be of likeness to that which is being fulfilled; there must be an affinity, a unity, a communion.

So we have this filling in Jesus Christ by whom we have grace and truth, the undeserved mercy and the reality. Grace and truth or the Gospel makes up the other side, the other supporter of the ladder. The Law on one side, the Gospel on the other, both from the same author, drawn from the same fountain, prompted by the same love, both fundamentally alike.

Humanity was making a failure under the Law. God knew it would before He gave it. The one supporter of the ladder was coming short of its purpose, not because of the weakness of God, but because of the weakness of men; because of man's wicked and sinful nature he could not perfectly keep the Law. A chronic disease had taken hold on man's soul which the Law could not cure. It could only pass the death sentence. The attitude which God always took toward man is found in the Law—that of love, good will, and prosperity. The fact that the Law passes a death sentence on the guilty is no evidence that it is not backed up by love. The same principle holds true in the mother who punishes her loved child for disobedience.

The fundamental purpose of the Law is to point humanity to God. The underlying principles of the Gospel are love, grace and redemption, making a way and pointing humanity back to God. The Gospel of grace is simply a more generous outpouring of God's mercy to man. Death's sentence was hanging over every human soul. God in His love and pity opened his store-house of mercy and love, poured out liberally His eternal grace and undeserved mercy to men.

Thus by Jesus Christ came grace and truth; by Jesus Christ the Law was fulfilled, a skeleton was clothed with life and truth; the weak places were strengthened, the breaches were closed, the Law was not destroyed but completed. As the artist with pencil in hand sketches the landscape, giving only a rough view of the scene, then turns with his brush and paint, not destroying the outline, not blotting it out, but simply filling the vacant places, covers the skeleton with reality; so Jesus Christ did not destroy the outline, did not destroy the skeleton, but simply fulfilled it, clothed it with reality, with His sacrifice and Gospel, making it complete.

The Gospel is just as needful as the Law and the Law just as needful as the Gospel. The outline just as necessary as the paint, the paint just as necessary as the outline, neither complete without the other. The lead taken from the earth, the paint taken from the earth, each containing like elements, used at different times and in different ways, yet for the same purpose—to complete the picture; the Law taken from a great treasury of God's love; the Gospel taken from the same treasury; each containing like elements used at different times and in different ways, yet for the same purpose—to point men heavenward, to complete the way and to perfect the ladder. The Old Testament explaining and substantiating the New; the New Testament explaining and substantiating the Old; the Law alone is not the way; the Gospel alone is not the way; but both combined form one perfect way from sinful earth to eternal glory. We do not combine the Law and the Gospel in the same way as we combine two different pails of water; but as we combine both sides of our ma-

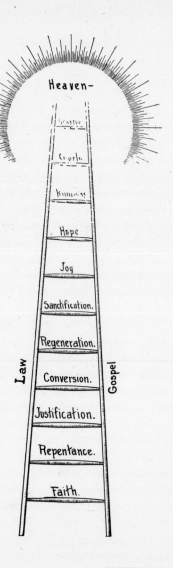

Heaven—

Glory

Glory

Knowledge

Hope

Joy

Sanctification.

Regeneration.

Conversion.

Justification.

Repentance.

Faith.

Law

Gospel

terial ladder with like material as the sides, so we unite the Old and New Testament, or

LAW AND GOSPEL

God is not essentially a God of division, but one of harmony and unity. The human mind in its weakness is in the habit of speaking of the Father, Son and Holy Ghost separately, while in reality they are a unit, "For there are three that bear record in heaven, the Father, the Word and the Holy Ghost; and these three are one."—John 5:7. "I and my Father are one."—John 10:30. One not in a material personality, but one in love, in spirit, in mind and in all things pertaining to man's salvation. In the face of this undeniable truth, why is it not also possible to unite, or rather leave united the Law and the Gospel which are simply a product of the Father and the Son? If they are one, surely their productions must be one. In reality, we cannot separate them. We must treat them as a unit, but for the sake of a more scientific explanation, I shall apparently separate the Law and Gospel and join them again with like material, drawn from the same forest, made by the same company,—Father, Son and Holy Spirit, making a complete ladder running from earth to heaven. I cannot say how many rounds in the ladder; neither does it matter for the present. We have already noticed that the Law and the Gospel are drawn from the same source, running unparallel yet used fundamentally for the same purpose. We shall now unite them with material drawn directly from each of them; material drawn from the Old as well as the New Testament. Notice only briefly a few rounds.

The first I find is Faith. It is a natural outgrowth from both Law and Gospel, Old and New Testament. The only means of salvation under the Law was not so much animal sacrifice, not so much temple worship, not so much tithing, but the great and important element was faith. Faith looking forward and believing God, believing His promises, believing in the common Redeemer, believing in Him as the salvation of Israel, believing what their eyes had not yet seen; the Law required faith. Without it there was no salvation. On the other side we need say little. The Gospel is full of faith. "By Grace are ye saved through Faith."—Eph. 2:5. "Without faith it is impossible to please Him."—Heb. 11:6. It is an essential element of both Law and Gospel; so we make it the first round in the ladder.

But one round never completes a ladder. A knowledge of sin, faith in the coming Messiah, was yet not sufficient. A second step is needful; knowledge and faith without repentance avail nothing. Repentance of sin was positively commanded and expected even under the Law. Nor was it put away when Christ presented His Gospel. It was only strengthened. "Except ye repent, ye shall all likewise perish." "Repent and believe the Gospel." Under the Law, as well as the Gospel, repentance was demanded and blessed, so we make it our second round.

"In the Lord shall all the seed of Israel be justified."—Isa. 45:25. "For not the hearers of the Law

are just before God, but the doers shall be justified."
—Rom. 2:13. "Therefore by the deeds of the law
shall no flesh be justified in his sight."—Rom. 3:20.
"Therefore we conclude that a man is justified by
faith without the deeds of the law."—Rom. 3:28.
It is not difficult to explain why there is no justification by the deeds of the Law. It is evident that
every man has broken the Law; hence there could be
no justification by it. Paul was not arguing that the
law perfectly kept would justify. He simply pre-
sents matters as they actually were. No man kept
the law and for that reason there was no justification. The secret to justification and salvation under
the law, Paul gives very clearly. It is "by the Law.
faith." Men were justified under the Law. The
Gospel is filled with justification so we make it our
third round.

Conversion, while not spoken of so forcibly in
the Law as in the Gospel, yet in it we see its underlying principles. Men, through the power of God
alone, seeing their sin, repenting and setting their
faces away fom the devil and turning towards God,
is conversion pure and simple. "Then will I teach
transgressors thy ways and sinners shall be converted unto thee."—Psa. 51:13. In the Gospel it is
most plainly taught: "Except ye be converted and
become as little children, ye shall not enter into the
kingdom of heaven."—Matt. 18:3. Conversion is
actually a part of the Law and the Gospel, and we
make it our fourth round in the ladder.

Man's nature under the Law did not change
under the Gospel. It is permanent. Regeneration,

which means being made again, made its first appearance under the Law. While it is generally not spoken of in so many words, it is, nevertheless, a condition resulting from repentance and conversion to God. He is a new creature; he is made over, hence regenerated. It was in the sight of God just as possible and acceptable under the Law as under Grace. From the Gospel standpoint, "Ye must be born again." There are no two ways, there is no substitute. Man must be made over and regenerated. He must start anew. So evidently, we draw our fifth round, Regeneration, from the same supply house—the Old and the New Testament.

Sanctification cannot be denied under the Law and less still under the Gospel. We acknowledge several kinds of sanctification, but the kind we shall use to join the ladder is the kind spoken of by Christ in His intercessory prayer. "Sanctify them through thy truth." It is the kind in which the Lord is the agent in accomplishing the condition, the kind which separates us from the world and sets up apart for special service, the kind that renews a right spirit within us, that starts our thoughts heavenward; a kind which can actually be reached, experienced and made practical. We find it in the Law, we find it in the Gospel, so we use it for the sixth round.

So far we have noticed only six of the essentials which join the Law and the Gospel, which are not foreign but natural to both. There are many more of which we have time only to speak in a general way, such as charity, humility, honesty, generosity, temperance, kindness, sincerity, joy, hope, etc., all drawn from the Law and Gospel. All essential parts of the way from earth to heaven, they clearly personify Jesus Christ, who was the Law, who kept the Law; who was the Gospel, who gave the Gospel; Jesus Christ the only way from earth to heaven.

In Jesus Christ we have the Law; He kept it perfectly. He kept it because it was a part of Himself. His mind, His will, His love, His life; He was wrapped up in humanity but His divine nature was never changed. In Him we have faith, repentance, justification, conversion, regeneration, sanctification and all our Christian graces. Man has broken the law, disobeyed the Gospel, has nothing of himself, but a glorious and undeserved secret is in this fact that through grace we have Jesus Christ, and in Him we have an unbroken Law, an unbroken Gospel; we have every round in the ladder. Surely "God is love," surely the way is clear. "The wayfaring men, though fools, shall not err therein."—Isa. 35:8.

My dear sinner friends, if you leave this place tonight without starting heavenward, I am sure you cannot lay the blame on God. It may be partly the fault of your preacher who has not set the ladder out clearly before you, but he has done his best in human weakness. It simply remains for you to act.

The way has been prepared, the heavens are open, invitation after invitation has been descending from the throne; you have spurned them all, you ask to be excused, you say, "Not now." "The way is hard." "I must leave my friends and I do not want to go alone." It is true the way leads up. The ladder is set on the earth. You must climb it, for it

runs heavenward. It goes upward always; its end
is glorious; it reaches even to God. The climbing
may appear hard but the Lord is our strength. The
way may seem lonely but we are not alone. We have
the love and sympathy of Christ; and more than
that, dear sinner, we are among the angels who are
day and night ascending and descending upon the
way administering to our wants. We invite you
again tonight to give God your heart and the angels
your hand and to set your weary feet upon the first
round, faith, and start on your way home. Come.
Will you start tonight?

"Have faith in God."—Christ.

"Now Faith is the substance of things hoped for, the evidence of things not seen."—Paul.

"By faith Abel offered unto God a more excellent sacrifice than Cain, by which he obtained witness that he was righteous. God testifying of his gifts, and by it he being dead yet speaketh."—Paul.

"Faith without works is like a bird without wings; though she may hop about upon the earth, she will never fly to heaven. But when both are joined together, then doth the soul mount up to her eternal rest."

FAITH

"He that cometh to God must believe that he is."—
Heb. 11:6.

The text this evening demands no argumentative truth. There are no two ways about it. Without faith and starting on faith men will never get back to God, any more than you could have reached this building this evening without faith in its existence and then acting according to your faith. Faith is the first step after hearing and knowing.

It matters not in what occupation you may take it, faith in the undertaking is always exercised. The capitalist who invests his thousands believes that he will gain a larger per cent. by it. The farmer who scatters broadcast the precious grain does it in full faith that he will reap more than double again. The horse trader when he contracts a trade has all confidence that he will better his material condition. The worst gambler or robber this world ever produced exercises an abundant supply of faith in his dishonest and ungodly business. The poorest beggar has faith that after all the world will not allow him to starve. He will always be able to beg his living. The honest, upright young men and women who undertake a college training have implicit confidence and faith that they will become stronger and more able to cope with life's problems than they could be otherwise. The world's most able writers dare not use their pen without an extra supply of faith. It matters not where we go, what condition or occupation we find, faith in a greater or less degree is at the foundation. When faith fails all else fails and passes away.

What seems most strange of all is to see people exercise faith in all material and earthly things, the drinking of the cup of cold water not excepted, and when it comes to spiritual things, the plan of salvation, the way from earth to heaven, the way of everlasting life, they say, "Give us a sign that we may know; give us sufficient evidence so we cannot doubt, we do not think it wise to risk it." They risk everything else in this uncertain world, take everything for granted, and never demand a single sign or proof. But when an eternal soul is at stake, they quibble and quibble, demand and demand signs and reasons until the devil has them so bound up and so blinded that all hope of redemption is gone. But just so faithless the human race has become.

On our pilgrimage from this sinful world to the Holy City, there is no one thing so important and comforting as faith. The reason is apparent. On our way upward we deal with spiritual and not material things. We deal with life, which to the human mind is a mystery. We see with the spiritual and not the physical eye. We travel on an unseen road to an unseen city. We cannot expect to see spiritual truth and understand the way with a carnal or physical eye. If that were possible faith would not be essential. But we deal with unseen things, with things "hoped for," and as Paul gave expression in his letter to the Hebrews, "Faith is the substance of things hoped for, the evidence of things not seen." It is after all what we hope for and hope to be that determines our course. That is what makes the way from earth to heaven so easy to know and to follow. It requires no financial capital; no honor or reputation, not so many diplomas or so many D. D's or Ph. D's; not so much intellect nor ignorance; not so much boasting of knowledge or ignorance, of humility or meekness; not so much Bible knowledge; but it does mean simple faith in the prepared way which is free and offered to all, the highest and the lowest.

We must not lose sight of the fact that

FAITH AND INTELLECT

are two different things. Where there is knowledge there is no need of faith. The less we know the greater our faith may be. No human mind can reach God; intellect goes part way but faith must complete the connection. Intellect and knowledge, to a certain degree must precede faith; but knowledge is not faith, neither can it take its place. Too many intellectual brains are making mistakes on this point. I do not condemn knowledge and intellect, God forbid. I only hope that people will wake up and put more time to intellectual development instead of continually condemning it. But I do contend that faith is not intellect, brain development alone is not faith. Intellect and knowledge have their part in producing faith but they can never take its place, any more than a fruit tree can be taken and eaten instead of the fruit. They are widely different yet very closely related. A certain amount of knowledge is necessary for faith as we shall notice later, but you may have a head running over with knowledge of all kinds, you may be able to quote the Bible from cover to cover, and yet have no faith at all in the salvation plan, as well as have a strong, hearty, beautiful fruit tree and yet no fruit. All our material things and our intellect and brain development, are good and necessary in their places, but they can never pass for faith. Faith is a gift from God and we receive that gift through hearing and knowing.—Rom. 10:17.

Faith that saves a lost soul is more than knowing that God exists. It implies a complete and unbroken trust and confidence in God. You need no faith especially to know that the sun rises in the East and sets in the West. You need no faith to convince you that two plus two equals four. You can see these things with your own eyes. But faith is required in unseen things; it requires faith to completely trust God, a Being who is not with us in person; One whom no eye can behold; One who is mysterious beyond all human intellect and imagination. It requires a simple, "Yes, Lord, I believe it, I accept it, I will obey it." Faith pure and simple, free to all who will have it.

Faith in God, or saving faith, means to acknowledge the Gospel of Jesus Christ the only plan of salvation and then act accordingly.

To believe God is to rely upon and have unhesitating and unfailing assurance of the truth of His testimony, and an unshaken confidence of the fulfillment of His promises, even though everything seems against them. It is simply taking God at His word with reference to His Gospel or the way from earth to heaven. If you believe it, if you have faith in it, you will be on the way. But just so long as men and women have faith in their own ways, their own moral works, their infidelity, their scepticism, universalism, unbelief and a catalogue of others, we cannot expect them to go on the Gospel way, and they need expect no salvation. It requires a faith which recognizes our lost condition; that earnestly desires salvation; one that will throw away all hopes in human inventions and accept the Lord's plan. The only genuine faith unto salvation we find in Paul's letter to the Romans, "If thou shalt confess with thy mouth the Lord Jesus, and shalt believe in thine heart that God hath raised him from the dead, thou shalt be saved. For with the heart man believeth unto righteousness; and with the mouth confession is made unto salvation."

It is evidently proved that faith may exist in

DIFFERENT DEGREES

One may have more faith than another. A believer may have more faith at one time than at another. Still this is no evidence of faithlessness. Some men have a greater caliber than others. Both may be full; the size of the vessel is not so much the question with God, but is the vessel full? How much are we overflowing? Our condition and environment determine our amount of faith. It surely requires more faith for a drunken wretch or some despised outcast to come to Christ than it does for a child who is just learning right and wrong. Saving faith is all of one kind—faith in the saving power of Christ, but it may exist in different degrees.

There are at least

THREE REQUISITES FOR FAITH

First, there must be a knowledge, in part at least, of past, present and future conditions. There must be a knowledge of an existing God who created all things; One who was from the beginning; One who sustains and controls the entire universe; One who created man pure and holy; One who knows the secrets of men's hearts; One who is all-powerful, all-knowing and everywhere present; a God who deserves worship and honor, One who is righteous and able to make man the same; a God who is love, who is life and who is eternal.

There must be a knowledge of Christ who was in the beginning with God; One who is in essence the same as God; One who is the only begotten Son of God; One who came to this sin-cursed world and paid our enormous debt of sin; One who bore our iniquities and suffered for us; One who did many wonderful works; One who spoke as no man ever spoke; One who died a painful death on the cross; One who arose the third day and finally ascended to heaven and is now interceding for humanity. There must be a knowledge of the fact that He must be the Redeemer of the world; One who has promised His Spirit who would convict the world of sin, of

righteousness, and of judgment to come; a Christ
who has promised to return and receive His people
home.

There must be a

KNOWLEDGE OF PREVIOUS SIN

A knowledge of the fact that though man was
created in a perfect, pure and holy condition, though
he had the privilege of remaining so and being a
glorious success and honor to God, yet he yielded to
Satan and made a failure. He yielded to temptation
and made himself impure and sinful. He has caused
sin and unholiness to pass down through these many
ages of time and adulterate every human heart.
Every man is guilty. "All have sinned and come short
of the glory of God." There must be a knowledge of
existing circumstances, of the unavoidable curse of
past sin; a knowledge of a tendency towards evil;
that Satan has been working against God in destroying souls while He has been trying to save them;
a knowledge of the fact that sin has never brought a
reward, but instead, has brought an everlasting curse.

Besides this there must be a

KNOWLEDGE OF PAST RIGHTEOUSNESS

With all of the devil's work, there have been righteous men and women. There has always been a spark
of righteousness even from Adam's time, though at
times burning very low. We must know that God
was continually teaching His people righteousness;
continually leading and trying to lead them into better
paths and more comfortable and more happy places.

There must be a knowledge of the fact that Jesus Christ by His life and words labored to make humanity more like God, to make us as nearly as possible what we originally were. The knowledge of past sin and righteousness need not be known completely but partially.

Before a saving faith can exist, there must also be a knowledge of present conditions. The sinner must know in part at least of the goodness of God. He must know that God is a God of mercy and not of anger; one who rejoices not over failures, nor delights in our sufferings, neither is pleased over the death of the wicked, but a God who is loving and kind; a God who delights in obedience rather than sacrifice; in righteousness rather than sorrowing, and in life rather than death.

Parallel with this there must be a

KNOWLEDGE OF INDIVIDUAL SIN AND GUILT

The sinner must know that he is weak and has actually sinned; that sin is weighing him down and that unless he is released, death will be the final result. He must acknowledge that he himself, and not some one else, especially, has done the wrong; that he is actually sinful and undone. He must confess with David that, "I have sinned against the Lord," and with the sinners on the day of Pentecost, "What shall we do?" He must know that he is lost before he can be found; lost to the world, to his duties and privileges; lost to the blessings and enjoyment of a Christian life; lost to all the beauties of this life, lost to God and the holy angels, lost to all that is pure and holy and lost to heaven. He must know that he is lost and wandering in the wilderness of Satan.

With this he must have a

KNOWLEDGE OF THE REDEMPTION PLAN

The way out from this awful wilderness. He needs to know that Jesus Christ has paid the debt and all he can do is to take Christ by Faith and cast his burden upon him. He must know that the Gospel plan is the only plan; that any man or woman who tries to get to heaven of himself, by his own good works, by his excuses, by other people's goodness or any other way than Jesus Christ, the same is a thief and a robber. The redemption plan of Christ must be known and acknowledged as the only way. Hearing and knowing God and Jesus Christ, knowing of the goodness of God and of individual sin, of our lost condition and the redemption plan are absolutely necessary before a saving faith can exist.

But still more is necessary. *There must be a knowledge and belief of a successful life of one who starts and travels on this Way from Earth to Heaven.*

There must be a knowledge that there is no success without faith; a knowledge that the very nature of faith and the way is success; that it is prosperous in every way. "Seek ye first the kingdom of God . . . . . and all these things shall be added unto you." It is a proposition of addition and not subtraction, as the sinner believes. It means wealth; it means unity and harmony with God; it means perfection and understanding; not a broken law; not a broken Gospel; not a conglomeration of principles. That is just the picture which the devil sets before the sinner and, too, very often before professors of Christianity.

Lastly, but not least, *there must be a partial knowledge of the future results of faith and no faith.*

A knowledge of reward and punishment. There must be some known ideal to which we expect to attain in the future; some result to be gained. We must know in part what Christ meant when he said, "I go to prepare a place for you." "Come ye blessed of my Father, inherit the kingdom prepared for you from the foundation of the world. And when he said, "Depart from me, ye cursed, into everlasting fire, prepared for the devil and his angels." There must be a knowledge that on the one hand there is eternal deliverance from sin, eternal happiness with God, Christ and the holy angels in an eternal home not made with hands; while on the other hand there is an eternal separation from God; continual remorse of conscience, eternally with the wicked, eternally with the devil and his angels, eternally in the lake which burneth with fire and brimstone. A knowledge of these things to a greater or less degree must be had before faith can truly exist.

THE NECESSITY OF FAITH

Naturally confronts us. I need not tell you that in climbing the material ladder we generally begin on the first round. The first round comes before a second or third. The effect and work of the first round always reaches to the top; so in climbing the ladder from earth to heaven, knowledge of the ladder, faith in the ladder, are the first steps and do not cease to exist until heaven is reached. The influence and work of faith passes through every round to the very top. The fact that under the law no man was justified save by the Law of faith, and in the Gospel the many references to faith, should prove to us beyond doubt its necessity.

But to make it clearer, it is necessary because it is one of

CHRIST'S PLAIN COMMANDS

"Have faith in God" (Mark 11:22). It was again repeated by John, "And this is His commandment that we should believe on the name of His Son, Jesus Christ" (I John 3:23). Having faith in God or Jesus Christ as the only way from earth to heaven is one of the simplest and most evident commands in the sacred volume. We have the word from the lips of the Son of God Himself, and there should be no question in our minds as to its necessity. Our real attitude should be, "God said it, I believe it, and that settles it."

But Christ was not satisfied to give the command only. He revealed to our own eyes some of the miraculous results of faith. The lame walked, the blind saw, the sick were healed and the dead raised. In the face of this plain commandment, and the results of obedience, do you dare ask, Why is faith necessary? And less yet, why do you dare to go and voluntarily break such a plain command? Disobedience to this command is the cause of all evil today. Faith is necessary because it is a plain command.

It was commanded and necessary because

"WITHOUT FAITH IT IS IMPOSSIBLE TO PLEASE HIM"

God does not make requirements for the sake of pleasure, as humanity does. He demands nothing that is undeserved. He demands nothing that is unreasonable. He does not desire to be pleased for His own sake alone but for the sake of lost humanity. He is pleased in seeing souls saved. Without faith no soul can be saved; hence without it, it is impossible to please Him. The very nature of God and His redemption plan proves the necessity of faith. On this pilgrimage of ours, we walk not by physical but by spiritual sight. If our physical eyes were sufficient, faith would be unnecessary, but since it is a spiritual way and not a material; since we cannot walk by sight; since God cannot be seen with the physical eye, it is very apparent why without faith it is impossible to please Him. It is impossible because the way is by way of faith, and to be without faith simply means to be without salvation. Without faith you cannot start on the way, and without continuing in faith, you cannot reach the top.

Faith, again, is first and necessary because

WITHOUT IT THERE CAN BE NO REMISSION OF SIN

"Through his name whosoever believeth in him shall receive remission of sins" (Acts 10:43). "Whom

God hath set forth to be a propitiation through faith in his blood to declare his righteousness for the remission of sins that are past through the forbearance of God" (Rom. 3:25). So long as sinners will stand back and say, "I don't believe in Christ, I don't believe that he will bear my sins, I don't believe it," just so long your sins will not be forgiven. Do not attempt to contradict God. Think for one moment. The power that called you into existence, and now holds your life in His hand, when He says there is no remission of sin without faith, the wise thing for you to do is to simply believe it, have faith in God and His provided way for redemption.

Finally, there is

No Eternal Life Without Faith

"Whosoever believeth should not perish but have everlasting life" (John 3:15). Eternal life is what God desires us to have, and He has made the way so plain and simple that we need be in no doubt. He might have made the way much more difficult and no accusation could have been brought against Him if He had, but because of the weakness of men He has prepared a plan for us; prepared a way by which the weakest of sinners may come; given it to us on condition that we have faith in Him; on condition that we believe on Jesus Christ. He has paid our debt, provided we believe in Him. He cancels no debt for the unrepentant and unfaithful. It is for those only who have faith in Him, and to have faith in Him means more than intellect; it means having a knowledge of Christ and of sin and of the redemp-

tion plan sufficient to submit, repent and obey God.
There may be faith, and yet no redemption. "Faith
without works is dead." A faith necessary for salvation must be accompanied by faithful works; actually
doing what God commands. Without faith there is
no salvation, no eternal reward, and no avoiding hell.

There is

No Substitute

For the first round. Nothing can take its place. I
see men refuse faith and in its place use their own sil-
ly inventions. They substitute unbelief, a defective
round which has no soundness, no divinity; one which
has nothing of God, and when they begin to climb and
attempt to place their weight upon the round, it gives
way; and in the last moment of life, when they desire
to escape the awfulness of hell and move away toward
the glory world, their own invention fails and eternal
death is the result.

I see others hewing down the Law and the Gospel
in order to fit their infidelity, their Christian Science,
"falsely so-called," they say the Bible is full of con-
tradictions and flaws, they say that it is unreasonable,
they say that Mrs. Eddy holds the true secret; that
sin, sickness and death in reality do not exist. They
plan their own invention by cutting away and ad-
ding to the ladder. I read, "If any man shall add unto
these things God shall add unto him the plagues that
are written in this book, and if any man shall take a-
way from the words of the book of this prophecy, God
shall take away his part out of the book of life and out
of the holy city" (Rev. 22:18-19). At their dying

hour, when they desire to cross over, they fall into an awful pit. Their plans are not of faith, their way is not divine.

I see men and women who make honor the first round. When the church and the world respect and honor them they will come. Again I read, "For that which is highly esteemed among men is an abomination in the sight of God." (Luke 16:15). I see men and women who will come when they "feel like it," making feeling the first round; just as ridiculous as for the starving man to say, "When I feel like it, when I feel all right, I will eat."

I see the moralist building on his good works. He says morality is sufficient. Christ says, "One thing thou lackest; come and follow me." "Ye must be born again." His moral works may reach the clouds, but they will never reach heaven. Only divinity can reach God. Only faith will satisfy God.

There is but

ONE WAY

Which leads from earth to heaven and that way is Jesus Christ. Faith in Him is the first step. Again to-night the heavens are opened and the angels of God are ascending and descending upon the Son of Man. Again the invitation is given to every wandering Jacob to have faith in God and be saved. Again the promises are handed out; promises of enjoyment in this life, of forgiveness, of redemption, of a glorious, eternal crown; promises for the highest and the lowest, on condition of simple faith in Jesus Christ. Will you accept tonight?

"Repent and believe the Gospel."—Christ.

"Mere sorrow, which weeps and sits still, is not repentance. Repentance is sorrow converted into action; into a movement toward a new and better life."—Vincent.

"True repentance consists in the heart being broken for the sin and broken from sin. Some often repent, yet never reform; they resemble a man traveling in a dangerous path, who frequently starts and stops, but never turns back."—Thornton.

"There is one case of deathbed repentance recorded, that of the penitent thief, that none should despair; and only one, that none should presume."—Augustine.

REPENTANCE

"Except ye repent, ye shall all likewise perish."—Luke 13:3.

Man is a free moral agent. He is living in a day of choice. Men may choose to live godly or ungodly lives, just as they will; God compels no man to decide or choose either way. He does, however, set before every wandering soul the way of life and death; the way of righteousness and unrighteousness; the conditions leading to each and the final result of each. He does not compel a single soul to accept or reject either way. He does more. He gives them intellect and reason; good judgment and will-power, and then invites them to the way of life. He invites every sinful soul to come and repent, come and receive rest, come by way of Jesus Christ, the only prepared way. But if they will not come, if they will not repent, if they will not accept, they shall all likewise perish. Man has his own choice now, repent and live, or refuse and die. Beyond the grave there will be no more choice. It will be death and only death. It matters not what you may think about it, that will not change the power of the text. There will be no alternative then; no more chance for repentance.

The supreme desire of our Savior was that all men everywhere should come to repentance. It is man's only hope for escape from death. "Except ye repent, ye shall all likewise perish." That means the unbelievers, the sceptic, the infidel, the agnostic, the atheist, the universalist, the spiritualist and every other "ist" who has not repented and been forgiven of God. Men may devise schemes of salvation, set up their own plans and inventions; they may make any excuse they please, may live moral lives, may come to church regularly, may pray long and loud, but "Except ye repent, ye shall all likewise perish." Repentance is one step on the way from earth to heaven which must be taken. There is no rest, no life and no heaven without it.

If this text were the product of some twentieth century D. D. there might then be some room for doubt as to whether or not repentance was an actual necessity. But the plain fact is, it is a product of Jesus Christ; the Son of God. The God who knows every human thought; the God who desires every human soul to be saved, and has actually prepared the way. Surely no man present can be so unreasonable, so foolish and light-hearted as to have the audacity to come forward and take a stand against God and doubt the necessity of repentance, or go so far even as many have and deny its necessity. Talk about the day of miracles being over. No! never: One of the greatest miracles ever known is being performed in the present day in the fact that God is allowing the ungodly, rebellious sinners to live; there can be no greater miracle than that of continual flow of mercy and grace to men who will deny and curse God.

We have no grounds whatever to doubt the

NECESSITY OF REPENTANCE

Jesus Christ, the Author of peace and rest, never would have given to man such teaching had repentance been unnecessary. To deny God's truth is simply an attempt to make a fool out of God and His Son Jesus Christ. My dear friends, what have you done? Have you denied the plain truths from the lips of a true, loving Savior? Is that your condition? "Except ye repent ye shall all likewise perish." Which will you have, repent and live, or refuse and perish? Today you may choose; today is the day of salvation. Tomorrow will be eternally too late for hundreds of sinners. Will you be one of them?

Repentance, strictly speaking, is more than simply sorrow for having done wrong. Sorrow is only one element in repentance. Very few people ever sin, but that they are sorry for it afterwards; but sorrow is not repentance. They are sorry, not so much because of the sin committed, but because their sin has been found out; because the world knows that they are guilty. I have met people who were weeping over their sin, but the weeping was because of its being known to the world. The adulterous are sorry and ashamed, not because of the sin committed, but because it was found out. The highway robber is sorry, not because of his deeds, but because he was caught and thrown behind the bars. Sinners the world over are more or less sorry, not for what they have done, but because the sin has found them out. Such a sorrow as that is not repentance. It is only rejoicing over sin committed and sorrowing because it has been found out.

Neither is actual sorrow for sin, whether known or unknown, accepted as repentance. I do not doubt in the least but that Judas was sorry both because he

betrayed his Master and because he was found out.
But that did not save him. He even "repented him-
himself," but what kind of repentance was it? It was
just what thousands of people today are trying to pass
off on the Lord and expecting salvation.

One thing we know, that is, if a man truly repents
to God he will not turn around and commit suicide.
That was the Judas kind of repentance. He was sorry
enough for what he had done, but he failed to repent
to God against whom he had sinned. He acknowledged his guilt to men, but there was no salvation in
that. God is the one against whom he had sinned, and
to God he should have repented and received pardon.

Thousands of sinners repent just like Judas. Men
and women see and acknowledge their sin against their
fellow men. Then even weep and sorrow their lives
away over their sin, but that is not repentance. David
might have sorrowed himself to the grave because of
his murderous acts toward the family of Uriah; but
had he not come and confessed that he had "sinned
against the Lord," he never would have been forgiven.
Repentance, which keeps a soul from perishing, is
more than being sorry for sin, more than telling
friends of our wrong, more than weeping and sorrowing about it. It requires a godly sorrow for sin committed. "For godly sorrow worketh repentance to
salvation, not to be repented of; but the sorrow of this
world worketh death" (II Cor. 7:10). True repentance consists in turning to God, confessing and forsaking sin.

It requires a sorrow and a repentance which goes

higher than man's head. Man can never reach heaven alone. Man may reach to the extent of godly sorrow and repentance, but the divine must complete the connection. It requires a coming together of human and divine before repentance necessary for salvation can be accomplished. So long as you, my sinner friends, keep sorrowing over your condition and repenting only to yourself and to your friends, you will never be forgiven. Priests may forgive you, men may forgive you; you may even forgive yourself, but unless you acknowledge your sin to the Lord and receive forgiveness from God, you still have no salvation, no promise of heaven.

Repentance which is followed by forgiveness and cleansing is made up of

A Sorrow for All Sin

whether known or unknown to the world; a sorrow, not because sin has been found out, but because of the deeds of sin itself; a knowledge of sinning against a powerful, just and loving God; a sorrow which reaches higher than man; it must reach heaven. It must reach Jesus Christ, the one in reality who has been sinned against. A sorrow like this is sure to work repentance.

It matters little how wicked a man may be, if he injures an innocent person in any way, as a rule, he has more or less sorrow, because he has sinned against one who has in no way offended him. At the same time, this sinner never sorrows in the least because he has sinned against "A friend that sticketh closer than a brother." One who loves him and has actually died that he might live. Only when sinners can be made to realize and acknowledge what they are doing, only when they have a godly sorrow for sin, can they expect to repent and be forgiven.

A godly sorrow and repentance for sin is not all. Something more is necessary. A sinner may repent every fifteen minutes, but unless he forsakes his sin, he still has no salvation. "If they pray towards this place and turn from the sin." Then only can there be a genuine repentance and forgiveness. It requires a turning away from and forsaking sin, actually having no more to do with it. So long as the sinner repents and in his heart is not willing to turn away and forsake all sinful desires and have no more fellowship with sin, he cannot have a genuine repentance and forgiveness. God knows every heart, and every secret. Not until all is given up, can a perfect work be done. There may be a "joining the church," a "Christian professor," but no genuine forgiven sinner, no saved soul.

When God requires you to forsake anything, He does it because He knows that thing to be destructive to your soul. I find sinners who stand back and refuse to repent and come to Christ because they say,

"I Have Too Much to Give Up"

"It takes away my liberty." You are mistaken there, dear soul. I want to ask you what you have to give up. You have nothing but a sinful life; nothing but filthy rags; nothing but sin and unrighteousness. God would not be just, would not be love, if He did not require you to give these up. He does it because He has something better for you. You are ignorant of the fact that you are only holding on to rank poison. You are ignorant of the fact that the very thing your soul is longing for is what the Lord has to give you.

What would you think of the mother who finds her child playing with a box of rough-on-rats, and when she attempts to take it away the child cries for it, and thinks it is giving up too much, and the mother allows the child to keep it and returns in a few moments and finds her child dead? What would you say of such a mother? My sinner friend, that thing which you refuse to give up is rank poison to your soul, and God knows it, and requires you to give it up. Physical death amounts to little. Spiritual death is death of everything and for eternity.

When you repent, you have nothing to give up but sin, poison to your soul. Why should you say you have too much to give up when the fact is you have nothing of value? God knows what He is doing and He will never require you to give up a single thing which will benefit your soul. He requires nothing of you but the poison.

Thousands are lying by the wayside, dead for this very reason. They started with good intentions, they repented to God of past sin, but they refuse to forsake sin. One or two pet sins they wanted to keep a while longer, and those very things have proven a curse to them. It has been poison to their souls and in an unexpected moment they fell dead by the wayside. Genuine repentance requires a forsaking of sin as well as an acknowledgment of it.

Turning and forsaking sin does not mean inde-

fectibility. It does not mean no more possibility of
falling and turning back into the world. It does not
mean that a man makes no more mistakes. It does
not mean "Once in grace always in grace," but it
does mean that there will be no more voluntary sinning so long as His seed remaineth in us. It means
that the heart is pure, and actually abhors that which
is evil. It means that a man will not sin voluntarily
and knowingly under any circumstances. When a
man repents and is forgiven, he is still human, still
wrapped up in human weakness, still subject to mistakes; only he has the blood of Christ applied to him,
his sins are covered, and he has the power of the Holy
Spirit to lead him and give him power over sin. Before he repented, he was the servant of sin, now he
is the victor over it.

A possibility of repentance does not come to men
just at any moment, mainly because of man's unwillingness. There are

SEVERAL CONDITIONS

which must precede. All of the things which we have
spoken of as prerequisite to faith must also precede
repentance, and especially must there be a knowledge
of sin committed. Unless the sinner is aware of his
sin, he is not likely to make any effort to repent. He
cannot. He must know that he has actually transgressed the laws of God, that he has rejected a loving
Savior, that he is hopelessly lost with nothing before
him but eternal death. When he knows this, he knows
enough to repent, and it is high time that he is at it.

I meet sinners frequently who take refuge behind their pretended ignorance of sin. There is no single excuse in this enlightened land of ours for ignorance, and in the words of the sacred volume, "The hail shall sweep away their refuge of lies and the waters overflow their hiding places." Show me a man or woman who says that they do not know that they are sinful persons and I will show you one who is guilty, and one also who knows it. This false pretense of ignorance of sin is one of the devil's best traps.

It is ridiculous for men to say that they are ignorant of their sin, when God has prepared a special way that man may know his guilt, as well as prepared a means of escape. It is worse than foolish for men to acknowledge that God has prepared a way out of sin, and not prepared a way also to show and convince a man that he is in sin. God is not so simple-minded as men. Any sinner who knows the way out of sin, also knows whether or not he is in sin. To know the way to your home is also knowing where you now are. If you can locate your home from where you are at present and know the way there, there can be no doubt but that you can also locate your present situation. The same is true of the sinner. He knows the end to be attained, he knows the way, and he also knows that he is a sinner.

Besides all this, God has provided

A Special Way

A way which never fails to convince a soul of his or her sin. "For if I go not away the Comforter will not come unto you; but if I depart, I will send Him

unto you. And when He is come He will reprove the
world of sin, and of righteousness, and of Judgment"
(John 16:7-8). Do you suppose for one moment that
God is so inconsistent and so weak in His sending the
Comforter or Holy Spirit into this world to reprove
the world of sin and then make a failure of His work?
Would you want to blame God for warning some sinners and showing them their condition and then overlook you? That way of reproving the world may do
for men, but God never does His work by halves. He
warns every man. "He commandeth all men everywhere to repent." His Spirit is everywhere and con-
victs all men, and that means you. Sin and guilt are
exposed. The way of salvation is plain. You dare
not plead ignorance of all these things. The lowest
heathen knows that he has sinned, though he has never
heard of Christ and His Spirit. Even if it were possible for you to be ignorant, your ignorance would not
save you; you are still lost. "Except ye repent ye
shall all likewise perish."

When the Holy Spirit has done His work, and
when God has shown to a sinner his sinful and lost
condition, the natural result is,

CONVICTION

Then comes that terrible burning of conscience; that
terrible remorse and heart-suffering; that awful burden of sin; a feeling of guilt; then comes the thought,
"O wretched man that I am; who shall deliver me?"
"My life is a burden; my life is a failure." As a
young man said to me not long ago, "Life is unpleasant, it is miserable, wretched in this condition."

Knowledge of transgression, conviction of sin; a terrible condition! But it is necessarry for repentance, it is God's love and mercy. He has made a way of escape.

Conviction does not always follow the knowledge of sin. I have met men and women who actually have no conviction. The Spirit of God has entirely left them. They have no remorse of conscience, life is no burden, it is no trouble. They simply exist like a beast, with no conviction.

I was tramping across a field some time ago with a gun on my shoulder. A flock of quail unexpectedly flew up at my feet; without a moment's thought I discharged both barrels into the flock. One bird fell stone dead to the ground and one was only crippled and started to flutter and run away. I paid no attention to the dead bird, but put all my efforts and energy to the one which was crippled. Listen, my sinner friend, that is the devil's plan exactly in capturing souls. You show me a man or a woman who has no conscience, no conviction, and I will show you the dead game. The devil has his work so completely done with them that he has no trouble to hold them. The devil is troubled about the crippled ones and not the dead.

There is no excuse for the soul without conviction. If such is the condition, it is not the fault of God. Conviction is a priceless gift which men receive from God, but like any other gift, men will squander it. They will so abuse their convictions that finally they fail to serve them any more. Then the cry comes, "O, if I could only have the conviction that I once had; I would gladly repent, but all is gone, no conscience, no conviction, no desire, I cannot come, nothing but death is before me." If you are laboring under conviction tonight, my lost friend, you had better repent, your conviction will not always last.

But having a knowledge and conviction of sin is not all that is necessary; unless you have

FAITH IN JESUS CHRIST

It will avail you nothing. A man is lost in the wilderness, and unable to find his way out. A friend meets him who at a former time had the same experience, but had been lead out safely. The friend points out to him the way and even offers to go with him and lead him out, but no; the man begins to make excuses. He cannot see his way clear. He is afraid he cannot hold out. He is afraid to trust the leader, and as a result of his fear and unfaithfulness, he dies in the wilderness.

Thousands of sinners are tonight wandering in the wilderness of sin. I ask them, "Do you know that you are a lost, wandering sinner?" They say, "Yes, I know it." I ask them, "Has not the Spirit of God been striving with you?" and with tears they say, "Yes, long ago." I ask them to come to Christ and let Him lead them out of this wilderness, and they say, "No; not tonight, I will sometime, but not now; I can't see my way clear, and I fear I could not hold out." So they will reject once more, and because of fear and a lack of faith in Jesus Christ, they wander farther and farther until finally they are eternally lost in the wilderness. Sinner, the Lord does not expect you to hold out. He does not expect you to see your way clear through. All He requires is faith and trust in God and He will do the rest.

Before a sinner can get back to God he must lay aside his fears and have faith in God and put his trust in Him. No sinner need be without faith and trust; it is free to all on condition that they are willing to receive it. No sinner will ever get rid of his burden of sin until he has faith in Jesus Christ, and that He can bear his burden of sin and forgive the same. Faith in Jesus Christ is a simple thing. It is really more than this sinful world deserves. We have no right nor grounds to doubt one moment Christ's plan of salvation. He knows all things and surely knows the way of our escape. When He says, "Have faith in God," He surely knows what He is talking about. Why should such a lump of weakness as you and I hesitate one moment to believe one who has called all things into existence! It is actually a deadly sin for men and women to disbelieve and mistrust Jesus Christ. "The fearful and unbelieving shall have their part in the lake of fire" (Rev. 21:8).

After the sinner arrives at a knowledge of sin, after he is actually under deep conviction, if he then has faith in Jesus Christ, one more thing is bound to result, and that is

Confession

Of sin to God. Now we have reached repentance. When you, lost souls, reach this point, you will repent. When you are so sorry for your sin that your sorrow actually pierces the celestial world and reaches the heart of God; when you are willing to confess before God and man that you have sinned and that you are lost and undone; when you are willing to call upon God for help and forgiveness, and are willing to forsake the world and all its sin, then you are near repentance, but not before.

At that moment there will be a wonderful change. One is actually surprised. "Old things have passed away and behold, all things have become new." Those great, dark mountains which the devil had stretched out before you all will have disappeared. Life will become new. That great burden of sin is taken away and you feel as though you could actually "Mount up with wings as eagles; you can run and not be weary; you can walk and not faint." There comes a great blessing, and instead of you giving up so much as you thought, you are receiving a thousand times more than you ever gave up or ever can. Instead of sorrow and disappointment, you will rejoice with the angels; for there is truly joy in heaven over one sinner that repenteth. Instead of your liberty being taken away as you thought, you now find that you never knew what liberty was. You now find that you were in bondage and only now you enjoy perfect liberty.

With very little reason it can be seen why

REPENTANCE IS NECESSARY

Before you can forgive your neighbor who has wronged you, it is first necessary for him to repent of his doings. You may have and should have that forgiving spirit, true enough; but that only clears you and not your neighbor. That does your neighbor no good whatever so far as his sin is concerned. His sin is still upon him, and always will be, until he comes and repents. With God and sinful men the same is true. God has that forgiving spirit always ready to forgive when the evil-doer is willing to come and repent. But that only clears God, and it does the transgressor no good at all and never will until he actually comes and begs for mercy in faith believing.

I need not tell you that without a genuine repentance there can be

No Pardon

For a perfect pardon, two things are absolutely necessary; first, there must be a loving, forgiving spirit in the one who has been sinned against, a perfect willingness to forgive, to love and have mercy upon the transgressor; second, there must be an acknowledgment of sin, a godly sorrow for sin, and faith in the one sinned against. There must be a perfect willingness on the part of both parties to forgive and to be forgiven. Only then can a true pardon be effected. It is one thing to get into sin and quite another to get out and be pardoned. A man will go strong-headed and will go apparently with boldness into sin, but when he comes out and is pardoned he becomes submissive and humiliated. There are no two ways about it; no repentance means no pardon; no pardon means no life, no salvation and no heaven.

Not only is there no pardon without repentance, but there is also

No Redemption

Redemption is one of the main cornerstones in the salvation plan. You may claim everything else, but "Except ye repent ye shall all likewise perish." Redemption is the only hope for every lost sinner. "Ye have sold yourselves for naught, and ye shall be redeemed without money" (Isa. 52:3). When the soul has wasted all, squandered all and given itself away for nothing, there is then but one hope and that is, it must be redeemed. The soul has nothing to bring, nothing to give in exchange, it must be saved and redeemed by the merits and good of some other. Jesus Christ has paid the debt. In Him the lost soul finds its redemption. It claims and has the promise of redemption on condition that it repent and believe the Gospel. There is no other condition, there is hope through no other than Jesus Christ who declares that, "Except ye repent ye shall all likewise perish." You may have your choice tonight. Which will you have, repent and live, or refuse and die?

It should be more than clear, even to the most simple mind, that where there is no pardon there is

No Eternal Life

Where sin has not been forgiven and forsaken, there can be no redemption, and where there is no pardon and redemption, there can be no eternal life. Repentance is not only necessary for the sake of pardon; not for the sake only of redemption, but most especially and essentially for eternal life. No sinner is justified in repenting simply for the sake of dodging hell fire; but he should repent for the sake of life. Men are called to prepare for life, not for death. The main essential which makes for life is repentance and forsaking of sin. Where there is no sin, there is life; and eternal life simply means to be free from sin. And the only means to be free is through repentance and forgiveness.

The burden of the preaching of John the Baptist was

REPENT! REPENT! REPENT!

In the ministry of Christ it was taken up with a double zeal and made clear above all things that without repentance there could be no eternal life. In the days of the apostles it was still continued, "Repent and be baptized every one of you, in the name of Jesus Christ" (Acts 2:38). Even to the present day the words are still heard from the lips of Jesus Christ the Son of God. "Repent and believe the Gospel." "Except ye repent ye shall all likewise perish." He is standing at the door of every sinner's heart with the everlasting message, "Repent." He is holding out before every one life and death and pleading that they choose life. Will you repent tonight? Receive pardon, receive redemption and eternal life.

"No," you say, "I will not repent tonight; I will wait for a more convenient time. I do not mean to reject my Savior; I only do not want to repent tonight." You simply mean to neglect. Yes, and to neglect to repent means nothing less than no forgiveness. No forgiveness means no less than no pardon, and no pardon simply means no salvation. I have learned that all I need to do in order to drift toward the deadly falls on the river, is to drop the oars and neglect them. All you need to do, my lost friend, is

to neglect to repent, and you will drift towards eternal
death as fast as the wheels of time can whirl. It is
only a matter of a few years, a few months, a few
days or a few hours until you will come sailing in at
death's door never again to depart.

You need not commit a murder or a suicide; you
need not steal or lie or commit any flagrant sin. You
only need to

NEGLECT

If it were possible for you from this day on to live a
life as pure and holy as the Son of God Himself, and
still neglect to repent of your past sin, you are still
hopeless, unforgiven and unsaved. "Except ye repent,
ye shall all likewise perish."

Thousands of sinners reform from many of their
wicked ways and live moral lives in the eyes of the
world. The reformed man is better in many respects
than the one who never reforms. Reformation is a
good thing so far as it goes; but it can never be passed
off for repentance. The reformed man who does not
repent is still a sinner. Reformation without repentance does not remove the condemnation of sin which
has been committed.

I met with a sinner a short time ago and he
frankly laid before me his sad condition. He said, "I
know I am a vile sinner. I am lost. I was once a devoted Christian. We had our regular daily prayer
and devotion in my home, but I have fallen away. My
children are growing up and confessing Christ as their
Savior and I am standing back a wretched sinner. I
had promised God some time ago while I was lying,

as I thought, upon my deathbed, that if He would have mercy upon me once more and raise me up, I would repent and confess Christ and serve Him faithfully. God actually healed me and restored me to my natural health, but I have neglected Him, I have broken all my promises. No one need tell me, I know what I have done, I know what I must do, the way is plain; the minister has warned and invited me time and again for years, but I have refused. I could not blame God if at any time He should call me off without a moment's warning because of my disobedience and neglect of what I know to be my duty. It is not a matter of knowing with me, but one of will and neglect. I often tremble with fear thinking there is no more hope for a sinner like me." But thank God, when this poor sinner threw himself upon the fathomless mercy of the Lord he was accepted and forgiven.

My lost friend, is such your condition? Are you neglecting what you well know to be your duty and privilege? Have you promised God to return to Him? Have you promised friends that you would turn to the Lord and then broke all your promises? All you need to do is neglect to repent and you will go drifting down the stream of time to the terrible falls of eternal death. Oh, the sin of neglect! Thousands of souls die unforgiven because they intended to repent but neglected. They did not mean to refuse and reject Christ, they only neglected, and as a result lost their souls.

Today is the day of choice; today you may repent and live; but what will be the judgment of the soul that neglects to repent! In that great day "every knee shall bow and every tongue shall confess." "As I live, saith the Lord, every knee shall bow to me and every tongue shall confess to God." There is a day coming when men will be honest. There will be another time when sinners will weep; a time when sinners will gladly repent, but the day of choice is past; there will be an honest hour but none in which to repent. The warning will go out no more, "Except ye repent ye shall all likewise perish." No more will be heard the message, "Repent and believe the Gospel." Then will be the time when every knee must bow and every tongue confess; but it will be no day of forgiveness. Then will be heard the cry, "O, if I only had repented; but now it is all too late; nothing left but a fearful judgment, and all because I neglected my opportunity. It was not because I wanted to, not because I was compelled to, not because there was no hope, but because I neglected." Oh, neglect! The devil's strongest trap! Come, sinner, and repent tonight.

Neglect of repentance means one other terrible condition. As a result of no pardon and a terrible judgment, there remains nothing less than

Eternal Punishment

A fire and brimstone hell. I shall not undertake to describe it now, the human mind cannot comprehend it in its fulness. We have but a faint idea of what hell really is, but that should be sufficient to turn any soul. Yet it is a fact that many sinners are virtually shaken over the very place, and still never repent.

How easy this place can be avoided if the plan is only not neglected.

In an eastern city a mother left her two children at home while she went several blocks to the store. While she was gone but a short time, when she returned her house was in flames. Her first thought was her children. Seeing or hearing nothing of them, she rushed to the back of the house only to see her loving children through a window on the upper story driven to the wall by the angry flames. While she called loudly for help, it was all too late and they were burned to ashes before her eyes. The awful agony of the mother can scarcely be expressed. Her whole mind was not so much on the fact that her home had been destroyed and her children burned alive, but on the awful thought, "It is my own carelessness, my own neglect, how easy it might have been avoided!"

I have not the least doubt that there will be cries in hell, "O, my own carelessness, my own fault, my own neglect, how easily I might have repented and been saved from this awful place!"

Tonight you have one more chance to avoid this place. Tonight you have your choice. Will you repent and live, or will you neglect and die? Tonight again the heavens are opened and the angels of God are ascending and descending upon the Son of man. Tonight the way from earth to heaven is again set at your feet. We hear again the tender pleadings of the Spirit to come. We hear again the intercession of the Mediator, Jesus Christ; we hear again the divine words, "Except ye repent ye shall all likewise perish."

We see again the angels weeping for you, lost one, and waiting to meet you, and to guide you on your way, and to send the message back to heaven to prepare another crown for another sinner who is coming.

Will you tonight while you may, accept Jesus Christ and His redemption plan and start on your way from earth to glory? Will you allow the angels to rejoice tonight over one more soul willing to repent? Will you cause joy in heaven which shall echo and re-echo throughout eternity? Will you repent?

> Some day, you say "I will seek the Lord,
> Some day I will make my choice;
> Some day, some day I will heed his word,
> And answer the Spirit's voice."
>
> God's time is now, for the days fly fast,
> And swiftly the seasons roll;
> Today is yours, it may be your last,
> Choose life for your priceless soul.
>
> Choose now, just now! there's a soul at stake!
> O what will your answer be?
> 'Tis life or death; and the choice you make,
> Is made for eternity.

"For by thy words thou shalt be justified, and by thy words thou shalt be condemned."—Christ.

"Therefore being justified by faith, we have peace with God through our Lord Jesus Christ."—Paul.

"And by him all that believe are justified from all things, from which ye could not be justified by the law of Moses."—Paul.

"To be perfectly just is an attitude of the Divine Nature; to be so to the utmost of our abilities, is the glory of man."

"Justice is the insurance we have on our lives and property, and obedience is the premium we pay for it."—Penn.

JUSTIFICATION

"In the Lord shall all the seed of Israel be justified, and shall glory."—Isa. 45:25.

Justification, in some form or other, is a universal desire. No man or woman feels comfortable when condemned. ALL seek justification of some form or other, either selfish or godly. I find people occasionally who comfort and justify themselves in the fact that they are willing to confess that they are unjustified in the sight of God. They feel a sense of justification in the fact that they are honest enough to confess their guilt. That is one kind of justification, but not the salvation kind; not the kind that eternally removes condemnation.

A few glimpses of our history and condition as a human race will soon open to our view the necessity of justification. Man in his original condition was not in a justified state. He needed no justification in the Garden of Eden. He was created perfect and free from a broken law, he was pure and holy; he was uncondemned, he had broken no law, had no necessity for justification. There was no broken law before the fall and without a broken law justification is uncalled for and cannot exist. Justification can be called in and used only when law is broken. Man's original condition was perfect, pure and holy as God Himself. Not until man destroyed his original perfection by transgressing God's laws; not until a broken law began to complain, could such a condition as justification be called for or exist. The broken law must now be satisfied.

I need not argue to convince you of

OUR PRESENT CONDITION

That man has broken the laws of God, has fallen from his original state of purity and holiness. Something must be done to satisfy a broken law. We are all guilty, "For all have sinned and come short of the glory of God." "There is none righteous, no not one." We have all gone wrong, we have all broken the law, we have all brought upon ourselves a condition which we ourselves cannot alter. We have not been obedient, and what we have done cannot be undone. There is no hope for us from a law standpoint, because we have all become transgessors, and by the law we are all condemned. "The soul that sinneth, it shall die." There is nothing left for us but death. Nothing else would satisfy the law. But at this point God, who is the Creator of all, the Originator of even the law itself, steps in and satisfies the broken instrument, the offended "schoolmaster," by saying that "In the Lord shall all the seed of Israel be justified." Now the law is satisfied. The Lord Himself must both live the law and must suffer the penalty, and in Him we are justified.

THREE PARTIES

are necessarily concerned before justification can be expected. First, God the universal Sovereign, the One who has been sinned against; second, man who has transgressed and broken the law of God; and

third, Christ who is our Advocate, who stands between God and man, the One who has satisfied the
broken law. Only through the harmonious efforts of
these three can justification be effected.

Justification, in the strictest sense, means to pronounce a man righteous and free from a broken law;
to release him from condemnation. The justification
effected by the three parties before mentioned, God,
Christ and sinful man, is in reality a free gift and a
definite work of God. It is not a question of good
works; works have nothing to do with it, only to
hinder when man puts his trust in them. We are not
justified by works of ourselves but by the works and
blood of Jesus Christ. The transgressor is released
from the penalty through the atonement of Jesus
Christ. On his willingness to repent and accept
Christ as his Redeemer, God pronounces him free and
uncondemned, and entitles him to the reward of an
unbroken law, eternal life. It is in reality a divine
intervention. Salvation is a universal desire, but cannot be obtained by man alone.

It is too late for man to be justified by keeping
the law. The law has been broken. "Therefore by
the deeds of the law there shall no flesh be justified
in his sight."—Rom. 3:20. "Cursed is every one that
continueth not in all things which are written in the
book of the law to do them."—Gal. 3:10. Man has
had one chance to justify himself by keeping the law.
But the moment the law was broken, at that moment
justication by the works became impossible. God
knew what He was doing when He gave the law to

man. The law would have satisfied God, provided it
would have been kept. No flesh was justified by the
deeds of the law, simply because no man ever kept it.
But there is where the difficulty lies. That is the reason why the law in itself was incomplete. No man
kept the law, "All have sinned;" not because they were
compelled to, but because they would. Since man has
brought upon himself such a sinful and weak condition, there is no hope of justification, no hope of satisfying a broken law, save through Divine intervention.

Man must be made just;

JUSTIFICATION IS ALL THAT IS LEFT

Not by keeping the law, not by making no more mistakes, not by attaining his original perfection. Any
one of these conditions would no doubt be acceptable
to God, but they are all impossible for man. The farther man goes on his own efforts, the farther he is separated from God. Something else must be done. Man
in reality does not become just. Some plan must be
devised in which God can accept him as just. He is
accepted, not because he is just, not because he is
good, but because in the Lord Jesus Christ we have
One who is just and in Him shall all the seed of Israel
be justified.

Man might work through eternity, but unless
God steps in, he never would be justified. Good works
are in themselves not condemned; but that never satisfied a broken law any more than the good promises
and good works of a horse thief would expiate his
former sin. The law must be satisfied; the penalty
must be paid. Man has made a failure in his effort in

trying to be good and do right. Works are not sufficient, because no man has the works. There is but
One who ever satisfied the law by works, "And by
Him all that believe are justified from all things, from
which ye could not be justified by the law of Moses."
—Acts 13:39. My sinner friend, if you hope to be
justified by keeping the law, by doing good works, you
had better give that up; for thousands upon thousands
of men and women who were stronger and more moral
than you have lost their souls and gone down unjustified, because they sought justification in works. Don't
try to justify yourself. Justification is the work of
God, not of man. You have no justification through
works. Accept the work of Jesus Christ. Let the
Lord justify you.

Neither is justification a combination of

WORKS AND FAITH

Works and faith are operated by the human, they are
man's part and cannot result in justification. "Therefore we conclude that a man is justified by faith without the deeds of the law."—Rom. 3:28. Not that
deeds are not necessary, but the point is, a man may
break the entire law and yet when he fulfills the proper
conditions, repents and accepts a substitute, he still
may be justified, not by the deeds of the law, because
they have all been broken, "But by the law of faith."
But he may be justified through One, Jesus Christ,
who has kept the law.

Faith and works go hand in hand. Faith without
works is dead, so are works without faith dead. But
men are justified, not by works, or deeds of the law,

but by faith in the One who kept the deeds of the law.

I hear some one say, "Why have a law then, if by the deeds of the law no flesh shall be justified?" Answer. Man would have been justified by the deeds of the law if he had only kept the law, but no man kept it; hence no justification. Then I hear the question, "If man is saved and justified without the deeds of the law, if it is only by the law of faith, why then do we preach faith and works both necessary?" Faith without works is like giving a hungry man a hot biscuit by faith; you may have plenty of faith in the biscuit but unless you perform the act literally it does the man's stomach no good. Faith without works is like a bird without wings. It may hop about upon the earth but it can never soar to heaven. So works without faith is dead. It takes both to ascend to heaven. Yet we are justified not by our works, not by faith and works combined, but by faith in the works of the Lord Jesus; the One over whom the law never held a condemnation.

"Do we then make void the law through faith? God forbid; yea, we establish the law."—Rom. 3:31. Christ came not to destroy the law, but to fulfil it. The fact that we are justified by faith without the deeds of the law is no argument against the law. It is really an argument for its establishment. Man has broken the law, Christ kept it and offended in no point. Now we can be justified only by the law of faith or faith in Jesus Christ, the only One who ever kept the law. It is evident that if Christ is the only One who ever kept the law, and faith in Him is man's only hope of justification, that surely the law is necessary and established beyond doubt, that faith only established the law and does not destroy it.

How people can throw away the law and refuse it is a mystery to me. Throw away the law and you virtually pluck out one eye. And it is no one's fault but yours if you cannot see clearly with the other. We need two sides to the ladder on which we climb. We need both sides of like material. If the law is a thing of the past, then Christ made a mistake when He kept it, and Isaiah was deceived when he said, "In the Lord shall all the seed of Israel be justified." The law is not made void, it is necessary. Christ kept it for us, and surely it was necessary, or He never would have kept it. When man is justified by the law of faith, it is because he has faith in Christ, and that means having faith in the law, and establishing, not making it void. It means that if man has Christ, he has the law and has it complete and hence is justified; justified not on his own merits but on the merits of Christ. After all is over, it is simply an undeserved gift from God. It is God's work that man is justified and not the work of man himself.

The work of man practically stops at repentance. So far every lost soul must go before being justified.

THE WORK OF GOD

now begins. The Lord can justify and forgive no one until the step of repentance has been fully taken. Sinful man must be willing to submit and repent. When this is done justification is also done, but it is done not by man, "It is God that justifieth."—Rom.

8:33. It is God who has been sinned against; it is Christ who is interceding for man; it is man who has sinned. The three parties are at their work. The sin-sick man is repenting and pleading for forgiveness. He has broken God's law and he knows that means death. But now he pleads for mercy. Now he sees his error and desires to be forgiven; desires to live right, but cannot; believes Christ can bear his burden, but somehow he gets no relief. But now Christ, his Advocate, comes before the King and intercedes for him; God's own Son is now pleading for poor fallen man. Surely, God cannot refuse One like His Son; One who has died that man might live. Surely, the heart of God will now be moved. If ever there were tears shed in heaven, I believe it is while Christ is pleading the case of a poor sinner. God cannot refuse, and when repentance has taken place and man has gone to his limit; when Christ, the Son of God, has plead for the sinner, then, "It is God that justifieth." It is now that God looks upon the work of His Son and accepts it. Now the law is satisfied. The broken-down places are not necessarily patched up, but Christ has the law unbroken, and sinful man receiving Christ, also receives an unbroken law. The sinner pleads for pardon, Christ advocates and God justifies. Now the sinner is pardoned and free from condemnation; now the law is satisfied; now God receives the man, not a sinner, but a righteous man; now He is ready to convert him.

> "Near, so very near to God,
> Nearer I cannot be;
> For in the person of His Son,
> I'm just as near as He.

"Dear, so very dear to God,
Dearer, I cannot be;
For in the person of His Son,
I'm just as dear as He."

While God justifies, it is also

A WORK OF GRACE

It is undeserved mercy. "Being justified freely by his grace through the redemption that is in Christ Jesus." —Rom. 3:24. It is more than the sinner deserves. It is more than the law allows. You may talk about justification so long as we live and still we cannot understand fully the grace of God in it. We hear it is, "Saved by grace"; we sing, "Saved by grace." It has become an old story. It is familiar to every tongue, and yet how few, if any, understand. It is not our own work, not our own way. "Being justified freely by his grace through the redemption that is in Christ Jesus." It is not by our repentance. Repentance and sorrow for sin is not justification. We are justified freely by "his grace." Not by works which we can do. "And if by grace then is it no more of works, otherwise grace is no more grace. But if it be of works then is it no more grace; otherwise work is no more work."—Rom. 11:6. More than sinful men deserve! I could not blame God had He compelled man to work out his salvation. He very easily could have found such a plan; but God is love, God is merciful and gracious and slow to anger, and because He is such, we are justified and redeemed by His grace— undeserved mercy.

The work of grace is made clearer when we remember that by the offense of one, judgment came

upon all men to condemnation, even so by the righteousness of one, the free gift came upon all men unto
the justification of life (Rom. 5:18). One man being
disobedient, one man breaking the law, has brought
judgment and condemnation upon all men. One man
having been placed in the most perfect circumstances,
yet of his own free will turned against the Lord, broke
His law and brought death upon all men; caused this
awful condition, not because he was compelled to, not
because he was so weak that he could not help himself, but because he voluntarily walked into it, voluntarily obeyed Satan and turned against God. But
with all this, man's meanness and disobedience, his
determination to destroy himself, "Even so

By the Righteousness of One

the free gift came upon all men unto justification of
life." Because there was One and only One who kept
the law, only One who was obedient to God; even
through His righteousness fallen man was justified.
Not because of our good work, not our righteousness
at all, but the righteousness and good works of Jesus
Christ.

Surely we are saved and justified by grace when
man may turn against God, and do all manner of unrighteousness, and afterwards repent and accept Jesus
Christ, and because Christ was righteous and just,
God grants to man the free gift—justification. He
receives sinful men and forgives them; they become
as acceptable to God as though they never had sinned.
My dear Christian people, have you really accepted
the righteousness of Jesus Christ? Do you claim Him

out and out, or only in a few things? Are you willing only to follow afar off? Are you sure that you are
actually justified because you have accepted the righteousness of Christ and that God has justified you because of this? Is the righteousness of Christ yours?
Sinner friend, have you been trying to be good, trying to keep the law? You may keep the law from
now on, but how about he time you broke it? You
cannot atone for that, neither can you mend it. The
fact remains, you have broken the law of God, and
you know that you cannot repair it. You know that
you have been unrighteous, you know also that there
is One, Jesus Christ, who never broke the law, who
was always righteous. Lastly, you know that if you
accept One like this who is righteous and has the law
unbroken, then and then only can you have the same;
only then will God accept you as justified. Do you
stand before God today justified or condemned?

Again turn to Romans 5:9 and find that, "Much
more then being now justified

By His Blood

we shall be saved from wrath through Him." In order that all righteousness may be fulfilled and the law
satisfied, there was required a shedding of blood, without which there could be no remission of sin. When
Christ took upon Himself the sin of the world, He
also took the responsibility of satisfying a broken law
which said, "The soul that sinneth it shall die."
Death was necessary. Shedding of blood was necessary. The blood of animals never could satisfy. The
blood of man would never satisfy. The blood of an

inferior could never atone for a superior. It required
the blood of One who was innocent and perfect, in
whom there was no guilt. It required the blood of the
Son of God before man could be redeemed.

When I see the three parties, God, Christ and the
sinner, in conference, the sinner repenting and accepting the blood of Christ, Christ Himself interceding in
behalf of the sinner, and God turning His face toward
the sinner and seeing Him under the blood of His own
Son, I hear the voice of God in loving tones, "Yes,
dear sinner, I will accept and forgive you, you shall
be to me from this on as the One who has never sinned." What a wonderful plan of justification through
the precious blood of the Son of God! How much
more blessed and sweet to be under the blood than
under the broken law; a burden of sin which will sink
you lower than the grave. Are you justified? Are
you under the blood? Has the blood of Christ been
shed in vain for you? Come now, get under the blood,
be justified and redeemed.

Will you follow me a little farther? The blood
of Christ was not all, nor the end. He was not only
righteous, not only condemned by sinful man, not only
taken down from the cross and buried, but He "was
delivered for our offenses, and was

RAISED AGAIN FOR OUR JUSTIFICATION

(Rom. 4:25). He died because Pilate was a sinner.
He was delivered because the Jews were sinners. He
was delivered because "All have sinned." To crown
it all, He "was raised again for our justification." A

dead Savior never could redeem. He must live and He does live. Jesus Christ, to the Roman Catholic, is only a baby and a dead Christ. A baby cannot hurt any one, neither can a dead man help any one. Our Savior lives again. He is just as real as ever. Thank God for a living Savior! If it were not so our redemption plan would all be in vain. He took His place in the grave because He was man and He took it again in rising because He was God. He arose, not for His own glory, not to convince the angry, hateful Jews, but for our justification.

In fulfilling His part of the contract which He entered into when He took the sin of the world, He was required to die. He was also required to rise again; and while He died for men, He also rose for men. He suffered the penalty and made a way of escape for us. He satisfied the broken law, paid our debt, rose from the dead for our justification. When you, my sinner friend, are willing to come to God and say, "Here I am Lord, I have broken Thy law, I must die unless something is done; I am willing to forsake my sin, I am willing to repent, I cannot help myself out of this awful place, the more I try the deeper I get in, but here is One the Son of God, He has been willing to carry my sin and has paid the debt; He has suffered, He has died. He has gone to the grave and rose again for me and I now accept Him, His blood, His righteousness to satisfy the law, to satisfy Thee." Only then can God receive you. Only then can He forgive you. Only then does Christ avail you anything. Then, and not before then, can you be forgiven, justified and uncondemned.

If you are justified by His resurrection, it is because you have given up and are willing that the old man be crucified and buried and a new life started. In the resurrection of your soul to life, you will be clothed with a new and everlasting garment. It shall not be material resurrection 'with you, but the resurrection of your dead soul. If Christ has not been raised from the dead, there then would have been no hope for your lost, dead soul; but He was raised for our justification.

But I hear a sinner say, "Oh, I can't understand, I can't see how this can be. How can a broken law be satisfied in such a way as you have been telling? How can God receive and justify a sinner like me? What good will it do for me to accept Christ even though He was righteous; even though He shed His innocent blood; even if He was raised again; I can't see, I can't understand."

You are honest, my friend, but that still does not clear up the matter, does not justify, does it? No, never. But it is clear why you cannot understand. The first reason is, you are in the dark, and how do you expect to see things which are in a lighted room while you are standing in one which is perfectly dark and have no means of seeing out? What you need before you can see is, first of all, to come from your dark room, come to the light and then you will see; the second reason Christ states very clearly. "If any man will do his will he shall know of the doctrine, whether it be of God."—Jno. 7:17. A third reason why you cannot understand, is the same why no man, though the most saintly, can fully understand. God never expected nor intended that you should. You need not understand all things about the Bible and the redemption plan. It is a wise plan of Gods that man cannot understand all things. If the devil can hold you back by making you believe there is nothing in it because you cannot understand, he is gaining his ends.

If such is your condition, here is a sure cure. God says, "Blessed is he that readeth, and they that hear the words of this prophecy, and keep those things which are written therein."—Rev. 1 :3. But He does not say that you must understand and see it all. God never intended that man in this life should understand and know everything, or He never would have said, "The just shall live by faith."—Heb. 10 :38.

The justified do not live on their understanding; not on their knowledge; not on what they are able to see, but they are justified and live through faith. While God expects as much intelligence of us as is possible for us to have, and while He looks upon willful ignorance as sin, yet God never expected us to understand Him in all things, but instead of understanding, He gave us a substitute which will do the same and better work than understanding. If you know much, it gives you so much less room for faith. If you know little, you have so much more room for faith, and, "The just shall live by faith." If you are unable to understand, you are just as sure of justification as the most intelligent; you have the advantage of the same faith; you may exercise just as much. All you need to know is that you are a sinner and that Christ is able to save you.

The old Jewish lawyers had a good knowledge of the law, but very little faith. Christ was unable to win them because of their unbelief; plenty of knowledge but no faith. He found the greatest success and faith among the ignorant and poorer classes, the fishermen, the farmers, and such like. The same is true today. Where Christ is most welcome, where faith is the strongest, you invariably find the poorer, the simple people. God does not expect you to understand all His plans, but He does expect you to exercise faith, and through faith you have life. "Seeing it is one God which shall justify the circumcision by faith and uncircumcision through faith."—Rom. 3:30. The Jews were saved and justified under the law, not because of keeping the law, "But by the law of faith." It was by faith looking forward to the reality, and not the type. The Gentiles, or those of the uncircumcision, are saved through faith. So it matters not whether Jew or Gentile, rich or poor, intelligent or ignorant, it requires faith for justification. We exercise faith. God exercises justice and justifies us.

To conclude it all, and put it beyond doubt or question, I quote from the Son of God Himself. Prophets may prophesy, apostles may teach, but no words are more certain than those from the lips of Christ Himself. When Christ spoke to the Jews he said, "He that heareth my words and believeth on Him that sent me hath everlasting life, and shall not come into condemnation; but is passed from death unto life."—John 5:24. Christ is the righteous One, the One who died, who arose again, who knows all things, and His solution is,

Believing On Him That Sent Me

It is not works, not trying; not knowing it all, but believing, having faith; and to make it certain, He says, if you believe you have everlasting life and you shall not come into condemnation but you have passed from death unto life.

Surely such a change must include justification. Can you doubt any longer? Will you linger any longer, my dear people, simply because you cannot understand? The Lord never asked you to understand all things. He asked you to have faith in God, and you shall be justified and when the time comes for you to understand, it will all be made plain. "For now we see through a glass darkly; but then face to face; now I know in part; but then shall I know even as also I am known."

There is no excuse for any one. All may be justified if they will. "God said so, I believe it, and that settles it." Will you take the simple plan and believe what you cannot understand? If you will, you shall be justified.

God does not require justification as one round or one step on our way from earth to heaven simply to give us trouble or to make the way hard, but for the opposite. It gets us out of trouble and makes the way easy. When we pass the step of justification, we can unite with Paul in word and experience that "There is therefore now no condemnation to them which are in Christ Jesus, who walk not after the flesh but after the spirit."—Rom. 8:1. There can be no removal of condemnation, no removal of guilt, no easy conscience until the law has been satisfied and the sinner is justified.

It is a sad fact that there is yet too often condemnation resting upon God's believing people. They feel miserable. They know there is something wrong. They have done something in which they are not justified, something which condemns them. They cannot feel that they are free from condemnation. They are in an unjustified state. There is only one hope for that class, and that is the hope of the sinner—repent, be forgiven and justified. The sum total of justification is the removal of guilt and condemnation; to place the sinner in a righteous, uncondemned condition.

Not only are we justified in order to be free from condemnation, but by "Being justified by his grace

We Should be Made Heirs

according to the hope of eternal life."—Titus 3:7. The final object of the redemption plan, of justification, is to make us heirs of eternal life; not to make us earn it, but that we may fall heirs to it, that we might be joint heirs with Christ. There is in reserve a great fortune, an eternal home not made with hands and through Christ, through justification, we may become heirs. It becomes a free gift, not only after we leave this present life, but it becomes so now. We have eternal life now. The moment we become justified, that moment we become heirs. Guilt is taken away, the penalty is taken away, and eternal life is the natural result. We become sons of God and not of the devil.

Then, finally, as a result of becoming free from condemnation and becoming heirs of salvation, we fall heir to another condition. It is an undeniable fact, we may be

GLORIFIED EVEN TODAY

"For whom he called, them He also justified, and whom He justified, them He also glorified."—Rom. 8:30. We cannot be so to the fullest extent, but when justified, we are also glorified. Now we only see through a glass darkly, but then face to face. Now we are glorified so far as possible in our humanity. We are now glorified in the fact that we are no longer guilty, no more condemned, no longer under sin, no longer guilty of a broken law, no longer the property of the devil. No longer are we slaves, but sons of God dwelling in a kingly palace, feasting at a kingly feast; wearing no longer our filthy rags of sin, but a robe of righteousness prepared by the King Himself. Instead of sin, we now have righteousness; instead of darkness, light, and life instead of death. Surely we are glorified even now. But if this is glorification—and it surely is—what will it be over yonder? "Beloved, now are we the sons of God, and it doth not yet appear what we shall be; but we know that, when he shall appear, we shall be like him; for we shall see him as he is."—I Jno. 3:2. My dear friends, you cannot afford to remain in an unjustified state, even for the good you may obtain in this life.

To obtain justification, I repeat,

TWO PRELIMINARY STEPS

must be taken. You must have faith in Christ and

you must sincerely repent of your sins. When you have done this, there will be joy in heaven because God will then do His part, which is to justify. That is the reason why He says if you pray, believe that you have it, and you shall receive it. It is all prepared, and the very moment you do your part, God's part will result. You cannot expect justification unless you fulfil every condition, and that means, empty out your entire heart. If you hold back one single thing, one secret sin, and are not willing to repent and forsake; not willing to make restitution where you have been dishonest and deceived any one, you can in no wise expect justification. If you are in trouble, if you think you have repented and you still are not justified, look up your back records and see if you have corrected every lie and made restitution in everything so far as it is possible for you to do. So long as you are not 'willing to do this, you never can be justified. Do not bother yourself about conversion, regeneration and sanctification until you stand justified before God.

My sinner friends, you also need justification. It is also for you. Do not think of being converted until you have repented and God has justified you. Then God will see to it that you will become converted. You repent and let God look after the rest. Do not worry, God will do His part. Justification is for you. You will meet it if you start on your way to heaven today. You will never find it so long as you keep breaking the law, keep traveling the downward road to ruin. Justification is not to be found on that way at all. It is found on only one way.

With all the darkness with which you may be

surrounded; however dark the night may be before you, however dark the future or the heavens may appear to you, however dark and thick the clouds may hang over your head; with all this in faith believing, lift up your long deluded eyes and you shall see the heavens still open, you shall see the Lord Jesus Christ, you shall see your own sinful condition, and again you shall see the way which leads from earth to heaven; the angels of God ascending and descending upon it; you shall hear the callings of God inviting you to come up higher, the tender intercession of a loving Saviour; you may hear the voice of some loved one calling for you, and before you allow the heavens to close, before God ceases his calling and Christ his pleading; before the way is taken down, I beg of you in the name of Christ to come and start for heaven. Repent, and believe the Gospel. Repent, and ye shall be justified. Come while you see the way; come while Christ still is the way; come while it is yet a truth and a reality that, "In the Lord shall all the seed of Israel be justified."

"The law of the Lord is perfect, converting the soul."
—David.

"When thou art converted, strengthen thy brethren."
—Christ.

"Conversion is a deep work, a heart work. It goes throughout the man, throughout the mind, throughout the members, throughout the entire life."

"Conversion is no repairing of the old building; but it takes all down and erects a new structure. The sincere Christian is quite a new fabric, from the foundation to the top-stone all new."—Alleine.

"When there is a sound conversion, then a man is wholly given unto God, body, soul and spirit. He regards not sin in his heart, but hath a respect for all God's commandments."

CONVERSION

"Except ye be converted, and become as little children, ye shall not enter into the kingdom of heaven."—Matt. 18:3.

No man was ever more positive in His declarations than Jesus Christ Himself. "Except ye repent ye shall all likewise perish." It is impossible to be otherwise. "Except ye be converted and become as little children, ye shall not enter into the kingdom of heaven." It is just as impossible for the impenitent or the unconverted to enter the kingdom of heaven as it is for God to lie. It cannot be. It is contrary to all spiritual laws. Why men and women try to enter the kingdom, try to climb from earth to heaven and refuse to repent and be converted, is a mystery to me.

If the way had not been made clear by Christ Himself, there might be some excuse for sinners. If there had been several ways prepared, there might have been an excuse for the impenitent; but since Jesus Christ, who knew all things, had all power, was so positive that there is but one way, and declared it more than once, there will be no hope for those who do not meet the conditions. If men want to miss heaven, they need only to refuse to take the prepared way which leads there.

In simple terms, to be converted means to be turned around. It matters not in what direction the individual is moving, when he turns squarely around and starts in an opposite direction, he is then converted from his former condition. He is now moving in direct opposition to what he formerly did. This is what we mean by conversion. We mean a turning around, a radical change in the individual.

It positively must be remembered that,

REPENTANCE IS NOT CONVERSION

Repentance is man's part of the work, but it is not conversion. John Smith is rushing at a break-neck speed down a mountain side, and it is told him to turn, that he is almost on the edge of a great precipice. Smith begins to repent and tells how sorry he is that he is nearing such a dangerous place, but goes straight on instead of turning. How much good does he receive from his repentance? How much good does it do him to tell how sorry he is that he is on such a dangerous road, or how sorry he is that he ever started that way, and yet does not turn? You at once say that it will do him no good at all. With all of his repentance and sorrow for his condition, that still will not save him, unless he is willing to be turned and to start in an opposite direction. It is a sad fact that hundreds of people comfort themselves with a kind of one-horse repentance and claim conversion. Repentance never was conversion and never will be. Conversion is God's part in redeeming and saving a soul. Never try to convert yourself spiritually; you may do it in material things, but not in the spiritual.

Neither is conversion

A CONFESSION OF WRONG

John Smith has confessed that he is on a dangerous

road; he has acknowledged his mistake; he confesses the result of such a course, but still is not converted, nor ever will be until he is willing to be turned around and started in the opposite direction. The convict behind the bars of the prison confesses that he has committed the murder, but at the same time is devising some plan to escape the law and repeat the act on others. With all his honest confession of wrong deeds, he still is not converted. How many times does the poor wretched drunkard confess his wrongs; how often does he confess that the drink habit is above all sin the most enslaving and sinful; how often does he weep and confess that he is worse than the lowest brute, but still he is not converted.

Men may confess and weep over their sin so long as life may last; they may confess every day that they are sinners, but not until they become willing to give up and be converted can they ever claim and experience conversion. God never converts a man until the man is willing to fulfil the proper conditions. Man must repent and confess his sin, but God does the converting.

I shall not be able this morning to give you all of the elements of conversion, but one of them we may be sure of, and that is,

A CHANGE OF MIND

"Be ye transformed by the renewing of your mind."— Rom. 12:2. It is not merely a change of outward appearance, but a change of mind. The old carnal mind is destroyed, and a new mind now exists. The drunken wretch, who becomes converted, now has a new mind. He is not only sorry for his sinful condition, but he has a mind now to be turned away from his sin. At first his mind was (though he knew it was wrong) to continue any way; but now his mind is new and he is determined to turn from those wicked ways. The ordinary, every-day sinner, when converted, is sorry, not only for his wickedness, but he now has a new mind which gives him new determinations. At first his mind was to sin anyway, though he knew it was unlawful, but now his mind is new and has become changed. As a natural result his life must follow his mind, for, "As a man thinketh so is he." Oh, the unrevealed power of a renewed mind! A mind which is in harmony and in touch with the Infinite! It may scale the highest mountain or descend into the lowest valley. How pitiful to see men and women staggering along with their old sinful minds, when a new mind is awaiting them. The converted soul tells many beautiful things, but the most beautiful cannot be expressed in words. The mind may scale the heights of the love and the divinity of God; but must descend again without any trophies for the world. There is no valley of disappointment and trial which is so deep but that the new mind is able to descend into it. Well may we realize why the love of God has so gone out for the world. His unlimited mind was able to go to the very lowest valley and sympathize with the most wretched sinner. Well may we rejoice today for the privilege of having a changed and a new mind. We do not deserve it but when we are converted we have it. Old things have passed away and all things have become new.

We may be certain of another element in conversion. With a new mind there must be

A NEW AND A CHANGED WILL

The old sinful will which was broken and of no service, is now become new, and while at first it gave way to temptation, had no power to resist, no power to overcome, it is now renewed and strengthened, and instead of yielding to sin, it has power to resist. There is nothing so shameful as to so abuse the will-power that it becomes ruined and helpless. Thousands of men and women in the present world who are respected and honored by the world, who in a few things seem to be strong, have their wills so dwarfed and ruined that they have no power to overcome their own lustful and sinful desires. Their wills are gone, and when the will is gone, the life is also gone.

Will you test your will this morning, my dear people? Are you disgusted with yourself? Have you given away again to sin and unrighteousness? Have you resolved and resolved again not to repeat those evil things, and just as often broken every resolve? I have a cure for you. There is only one remedy. No man has a patent on it, either. It is free to all who will receive it. If you will take a few minutes of faith in God, well mixed with a few minutes of genuine repentance, you will be restored completely. You will be converted, and that consumptive will of yours will become robust and strong, will become new and able to conduct your life properly.

With a new mind and a new will, we are sure of another condition, and that is,

A New Desire

The sinner in a sense has no desire for sin. He desires to do good. He would rather be free from sin. He would rather be a Christian. He desires a happier experience. All this he will confess, but the fact still remains, that after all, the desire is more to continue in sin. His desires lead him to satisfy his carnal nature, his evil inclinations, his perverted will; in reality, he desires to satisfy the devil who is leading him. His desires largely run along unrighteous lines. But when a soul is actually converted, he will not only desire to do good, to be free from sin; will not only desire to have a happier experience, but all these things he will have and it will be a real desire; a sincere desire; one which will lead toward righteousness. The new desire will be for Gospel truths, for spiritual things, for the welfare of all men. There will be a hunger for different food. Old desires will pass away and all will become new.

One more element, we may rightly conclude. With a new mind, a new will and new desires, as a natural result there must be

A New Life

The old man is gone, the new man is now in existence. The old sinful life is no more, but a new life now exists. There can be nothing more honorable to God than a combination of a new mind, a new will, a new desire, and a new life. Surely it was worth while to become converted. Surely it is nothing unreasonable or unjust. How different the world appears; how different God appears; how different everything appears? In all things there is beauty. From every condition we draw something good. No condition will discourage us for, "We know that all things work together for good to them that love God, to them who are the called according to his purpose."—Rom. 8:28. There will be no false accusations, no fault-finding, no grumbling, no neighborhood gossip. There will be better things to occupy the mind. There will be nobler thoughts to consider, nobler deeds to perform. There will result a life which will become a light to the world; a life worthy of example, a life worth living, and last of all and most important, a life which will live through the continuous ages of eternity; one which shall live in happiness and rest so long as God and eternity last.

Before we proceed further, I shall invite your attention to a few

PRELIMINARY CONDITIONS OF CONVERSION

Several times have you been reminded that conversion is the work of God. No man can be converted unless the Father draw him (Jno. 6:44). But while this is the work of God, it yet demands that man fulfil a condition. The conversion plan is already prepared. And the moment man is willing to do his part the work is done. No man who stands back and demands of God to save him, if he wants him to be saved, will ever be converted. I have heard men claim that God placed them in this world and now He might save them if He wants them saved. There is no salvation for such a condition. I have heard men say that they are too sinful, the Lord cannot bear their

sin. There is no salvation to that class. There must
be a complete faith in Christ, who has paid the debt,
provided we are willing to accept this plan. It is inconsistent for a man to desire conversion and at the
same time have no faith in the plan. Man's part is
having faith. God does not demand perfect knowledge, but faith in Christ, and it may be had by all
who know His name. Faith is the first step on the
way; it is one preliminary condition.

With genuine faith another condition comes in
before conversion, and that is a sickness of sin. Where
a sinner does not realize his disease, his filthy condition; where he is not sick and tired of himself; where
he does not see death staring him in the face, there is
little hope of conversion. Often have I been made to
rejoice when I saw people so sick of themselves that
they knew no more what to do or where to go. I enjoy it, not because I like to see them so miserable, but
because they are now coming near the kingdom. I
have met people in my brief evangelistic experience
who were sick and confined to their beds; but upon investigation it was not a sickness from some physical
defects, but a sickness resulting from sin.

On one special occasion I was called to visit a
certain sinner who was sick in bed. I soon saw what
the trouble was. I began to talk Gospel, repentance
and judgment to come, and soon there was a change in
conditions. That same evening this sick sinner came
to the meeting and confessed Christ, and the sickness
left entirely.

I see men who are professional grumblers. The
dinner never is right; the supper never is right; the

breakfast never is right; they must always have a side
dish of toast or dainties specially prepared, because
they have "stomach trouble," so-called. Nothing
agrees with them. It is a natural result: that angry
and disturbed brain will affect the stomach.

There are also cases where special dishes must
be prepared. The physical man will wear out, but if
seventy-five per cent. of our men and women would
repent of their ungodliness there would not be one
case of sickness and stomach trouble where there are
ten this way. Shame on you old grumblers that can't
eat a meal without finding fault and setting up a
howl. You can make a glutton of yourselves when it
comes to some other man's table, or when it comes to
tobacco or beer, but at home you are as mean and angry as a bear with a sore head. Shame on you! What
you need, instead of toast and dainties, is a genuine
repentance and conversion. I hope you do get sick
and so seriously sick of yourselves that you will repent and be converted.

When you have faith in Christ and are sick of
yourself and are willing and do repent, you have done
your part. When you have done this you will be converted. The Lord has done his part and is waiting
for you to do yours. So long as you stand and wait
for God to do your part, you will never be converted.
Do not expect to get to heaven without doing something yourself. You have very little to do at best;
there is very little that you can do; but God expects
you to do it just the same. How can you be so lazy
as to want to get to heaven and do nothing? You

can do little enough when you do all that is in your power to do. You must comply with the conditions preliminary to conversion. Then the Lord will see to it that you are perfectly converted.

Only one moment's thought will bring to our mind

THE ENORMOUS WORK OF CONVERSION

When we think of the powers concerned; God, the Creator of all; the devil, the perverter of all, so far as it is in his power, and a lost soul standing between the two, knowing that one of the two powers shall win, one for eternal rest, the other for eternal damnation; no soul can ever be won from these inducements of Satan to be saved but alone through the

POWER OF GOD

I do not wonder at Christ's own words, "No man can come to me except the Father which hath sent me draw him." Thousands of sinners die annually through the false idea that when they get ready once, they will repent and be converted. They do not think that there may be a time when they are ready that the Father is not. They fail to realize that while the Father is drawing is their only time to come. They never can come on any other condition, only that the Father is drawing. They may want to repent and come ever so much, but unless the Father is drawing, there is no hope for them. The devil is different; he never gives up trying and drawing. What a sad condition it must be for those who have a desire to come but the Father no longer draws them. "My spirit," He says, "shall not always strive with man." My friends, if you feel that God is drawing you today, the wise thing for you to do is to submit. You do not know how long the Lord will strive with you. Tomorrow may be forever too late for you. While you may think that tomorrow you will be ready, it may be you will, but it may be also that the Lord will not.

A young man left the services one evening, saying that if he felt the next evening as he did then, he would confess Christ. The next morning he was found dead in his bedroom. The Lord was ready, but he was not. Why do sinners act so foolishly? Think one moment, and you will realize that the Lord is not drawing you for nothing. It means something when the Lord begins to draw and to call you to come up higher. He knows best the danger with which you are surrounded. He knows best how near the devil has you in his eternal clutches. He knows how near you stand to your grave. He knows how near you stand to the threshold of eternity. Will you not come today? Will you let the Lord have his way? He has a purpose in drawing you. Some of you sinners attend these services day after day, night after night, and it takes all the strength within you to keep from coming to God. Now it takes all the strength you have to refuse Him. The day is not far distant when with all the power you have you cannot accept Him. Leave these foolish ways of yours, and while the Lord is merciful enough to you to draw you, do not refuse Him. The time will soon be when you will see how foolish you were but it will then be too late. What is done cannot be undone. Then will be heard the weeping and calling for one more drawing from God; for one more chance to come; and the answer may be heard, "The days of grace are over, many days and calls you have refused, there now is no hope for you, depart from me, I never knew you." That will be a sad day for you, my sinner friends. Today you may engage in your foolishness; today you may fight your conviction; today you may refuse the Lord, trample his calls and drawings beneath your feet; today you may say as did a sinner to me, on the streets of Chicago, "D——n Jesus Christ," but at that day you will weep; then you will realize when too late, that you are damned and not Jesus Christ. Then you will plead for mercy, but you shall not be heard. We beg of you, come today. Come while the Father is drawing and doing His work.

But the Father is not satisfied with His efforts alone. He is anxious for your salvation that "Having

Raised up His Son Jesus

sent Him to bless you in turning away every one of you from his iniquities."—Acts 3:26. It matters little how wicked a man may be, if he can get one view of Jesus Christ, he is sure to turn from his sins. The life and righteousness of Christ is unequaled by any character that the world has ever produced. Many have been the moral characters; many have been our honest, upright and honorable men, but none has there yet been who has never failed; who has never sinned or made a mistake, save Jesus Christ. He is the central figure of the whole world, as well as the central figure of the Bible. There is no righteousness or perfection like His. Enemies as well as friends confess to His righteousness. The Pharisees, rulers and devils all with one accord declare that he is the "Son of David;" "I find no fault in this man." They even "believe and tremble." The testimonies even reach the celestial world and the angels and God Himself give testimony to the righteousness of Jesus Christ. It is not a miracle that one view of such a character is able to turn sinners from their sin. It is only a natural result when a soul sees the righteousness of another to desire to become like it.

The kindness of Christ won and converted many sinners. Though shamefully abused and spoken against, He was kind and sympathetic. No soul so lowly, no sinner so degraded but that Christ had sympathy and kind words for him. Any man can aid and stand by the rich and the honorable, the well-to-do; any man can sacrifice for his superiors or equals, but very few like Christ can stoop to the very lowest, and in loving, heart-searching words lift them out of their awful condition. Only Christ can come to lost men who have spent years in sinning against Him and say, "Thy sins are forgiven thee." Only Christ is so kind as to notice the decaying leper and pronounce him clean. Only Christ can look upon blind Bartimeus and restore his sight. What a wonderful character of kindness! Not only was he unlimited in his kindness to present conditions, but it even pierced the very grave and brought forth the dead. Weeping sisters were made to rejoice over a risen Lazarus. Weeping mothers over the raising of dead sons and daughters.

No man ever died in the presence of Christ. Every funeral was broken up which He attended. What acts of kindness! Can any sinner be so stony-hearted as not to be moved to turn from his sin and come to a Savior like that? Surely the kindness of Christ has been the means of "Turning away every one of you from your iniquities."

But the crowning work of the Redeemer's life may be seen in

His Final Victory

No man or woman, however sinful, can behold Him in this act and not be moved to repentance. The world has no place for Christ; it is against Him without cause. Sinful men are oppressing and falsely accusing Him. They cannot rest when they see his righteousness and His kindness. They unlawfully lead Him before ungodly rulers for condemnation. They are determined to work Him away to the grave. They, without a single just cause, lead Him to Calvary. They nail Him to a cruel cross and erect it between two thieves signifying that he is the chief sinner. They watch Him there. They mock and ridicule Him. They drive a spear into His side and finally satisfy themselves that this "blasphemer," this "imposter" is out of their way. They take Him down from the cross and carry Him to the grave, and when He is laid away, they roll a great stone to the door of the sepulcher and depart. But for fear of what He had often said, that He would rise on the third day, the chief priests and Pharisees came to Pilate saying, "We remember that that deceiver said while he was yet alive, after three days I will rise again; command therefore that the sepulcher be made sure until the third day lest his disciples come by night and steal him away and say unto the people, He is risen from the dead, so the last error shall be worse than the first."—Matt. 27:62-64.

Pilate consented and told them to take their watch and go their way and make the sepulcher as sure as possible, and they went, "And made the sepulcher sure, sealing the stone, and setting a watch." Apparently the angry Jews are now satisfied. This deceiver is out of our way. He claimed to be the Son of God; He claimed that He could destroy the temple and build it in three days but He has failed in it all. In the eyes of the world He has made a shameful failure. His work is done; He is in the grave there to decay like all men. The grave is made sure—but to the surprise of all men, to the surprise of the guards who even became as dead men—the sepulcher was thrown open, and on the morning of the third day the Son of man came forth. He came without consent of the watch; regardless of the king's seal. The stone was rolled away, not to let Him out of the grave, but to convince the world that He was out. He broke every band of death; nothing could hold Him, and this condition, which in the eyes of the world was a defeat to Christ and a victory to them, turned on a pivot and made a shameful defeat to the world and a glorious victory to the Son of God. Thank God, our Redeemer lives!

You may speak of your Caesars and Napoleons; of your bloody victories on land or sea, but no victory has ever equaled, or ever will equal, the victory of Jesus Christ over death and His enemies. Any man can die facing the most deadly enemy, the hottest storm of bullets; any hero may go down to his grave, but none but the Son of man can again come forth on the third day. No victory like Christ in the resurrection. No sinner can behold this wonderful victory, and what it means to him, without a strong desire to turn from his wicked ways. How condemned the sinner feels when he realizes that he is refusing such a Savior as Jesus Christ.

I cannot doubt that Peter knew what he was talking about when he represented Jesus Christ as the One who would turn sinners from their iniquities. No one knew so well what it meant as Peter, himself at an earlier time a sinner and several times even denied Christ. He allowed himself to be scared out of his religion by a girl, yet he knew that Jesus Christ was able to turn men from their wicked ways. It does seem strange today how men and women can stand in their sins when they have placed before them the righteousness of one like Christ. How can they refuse to repent when they know of the wonderful kindness of one like Jesus Christ? How can they put off their salvation another day when they see the marvelous victory of the Son of man?

I have had men to tell me that they had no heart; and I have almost come to the conclusion that it was actually the case with some. When I see people so wonderfully blessed with this world's goods, with good health and with friends; when they have the

Son of God placed so vividly before them and yet do not think it worth the while to thank the Lord for it, and are not serious enough to turn away from their sin and wickedness and come to Christ and be converted, I must believe that either they have no heart, or if they have one, it is so small and shriveled that it cannot be found. No whole hearted person knowing these things will stay away from Christ.

But I find another agent in our conversion. Solomon gives voice to it in Proverbs 1:23. "Turn you at my reproof;

BEHOLD I WILL POUR OUT MY SPIRIT

unto you, I will make known my words unto you." I have now found that the Father, Jesus Christ, and the Holy Spirit necessarily enter into our conversion. It is impossible for man to convert himself. The Holy Spirit, who is given to reprove the world of sin, to turn us from our evil ways and to lead us into all truth, is to sinners a God-sent gift. No soul can turn from sin until it knows its sin, until it is convicted of sin, until the way of truth and righteousness is revealed. Men excuse themselves many times upon the grounds of their ignorance. They say that they do not know they are sinners. They expect to be saved upon their ignorance. It would be just as reasonable for a man to remain in a burning building and expect to be saved because he was ignorant of the fire. His ignorance will never save him, neither will ignorance excuse any sinner at the judgment. "And the times of this ignorance God winked at: but now commandeth all men everywhere to repent."—Acts 17:30. It is not my duty to interfere with God's former doings with men; but I do know that now, "He commandeth all men everywhere to repent," and I know this means every sinner in this building. I know that the Holy Spirit is doing His work in reproving the sinner; I know He is warning you, convicting you; I know He has revealed to you that you are a sinner, because I know that God never lies, and He has said that His Spirit would reprove the world of sin. He said that He commandeth all men everywhere to repent. I know that, "The grace of God that bringeth salvation hath appeared to all men; teaching us that, denying ungodliness and worldly lusts, we should live soberly, righteously and godly in this present world." —Titus 2:11, 12. My dear people, "Let God be true and every man a liar." Let no sinner say that the Spirit has never warned Him. Let no sinner attempt to make a stand against Him. It never pays. Be honest today, if you never have been before. Confess today, if you never have before, that the Father is drawing you, that the life of Christ is worthy of example, and that the Holy Spirit is calling you. What you need is to submit and yield yourself to God and conversion will be the result.

A genuine conversion will be known. Anything that does not change a sinful man cannot be called conversion. Anything which does not make him a different man or does not animate him to

Make Restitution

so far as possible is not conversion. When a sinner is converted, the neighborhood will know it. There will be things revealed never before known. When Zaccheus climbed the sycamore tree as Christ was passing by, he was a sinner. He was chief among the publicans. He was rich. He wanted to see Jesus. While he was in the tree he saw Him and Jesus saw him, spoke to him and invited him down. The first thing Christ does is to invite the sinner to come down. The second thing, He invites him to come up. How is it with you, lost soul? Have the eyes of Christ fallen upon you? Have you been invited down? Zaccheus came down but he was a different man than he was when he climbed the tree. Something happened during the time he left the tree until he struck the ground. He talks differently now. Listen what he says. "Behold, Lord, the half of my goods I give to the poor and if I have taken anything from any man by false accusation, I restore him four fold."—Luke 19:8. No one needs to proclaim it over the country that something has happened with Zaccheus. He was entirely different and was not ashamed to confess that he had wronged some and that he would make restitution.

I have very little confidence in a conversion where no restitution is made at all. Some have more, and others less. The old professional sinner, when converted, will, without question, have more restitution to make than the young soul who is just learning right from wrong and is converted. The child may remember or have nothing to make restitution for. He has just come to the parting of the way and consequently by taking the Lord's way, there is no call for restitution. But I have found no professional

sinner who could say that he knew of nothing in his
past sinful life which he could not, in part at least,
correct. I find none who can say that they have always been strictly honest and never deceived any one,
either in word or deed. I find none who can say that
they know of no wrong which they could not right in
part by going to the party and confessing and restor-
ing.

It is utterly impossible to have a genuine conversion without restitution. When a sinner gets so
thoroughly converted that he will work for months
and years to pay up his back debts and stolen things,
you may be certain that something has taken place
similar to that in the life of Zaccheus. When I see
men borrowing money and even selling off their needed personal property for the special purpose of making restitution for false gain, I am satisfied in my
mind that a change has taken place. I am further satisfied that though it takes all a man has to make restitution, even his house and home, the Lord will care
for such a man. He will never starve. Restitution is
only a natural result of conversion. It is one of the
most evident marks of a changed life.

How men can be converted and no one ever
know it is a problem yet unsolved. How men can
make wrongs right and it not be known is something
I have never learned. My Bible tells me that a thief
shall restore four and five times as much as he stole
(Exodus 22:1). It is a plain, positive command, and
has never been altered. It matters not how small the
article may be, if it is stolen, it is stolen, and you may

repent and repent, and if you are unwilling to re-store so far as possible, your repentance will do you no good. The Lord never will do anything for you which you can do yourself. He will never carry home stolen chickens or stolen watermelons. You can do that yourself. The Lord demands it of you and not until you are willing to do it can you experience true conversion. You cannot enjoy your trip on the way from earth to heaven knowing that you have in your possession things falsely gained.

I know some of you people who claim conver-sion say that restitution is unnecessary. If we repent and reform, that is sufficient. The Bible does not say so. It does say repent (Mark 1:25), and restore (Ex-odus 22:1), and you had better not set yourself up against God. You had better not add anything to or take away anything from the Bible. You say it is hard to make restitution. I am ashamed to reveal the things of which I am guilty. That is only natur-al. If you were not ashamed of yourself when you deceived your neighbor or friend, you must be now. It is only natural because it is a shame. If you had been ashamed at the right time, you now would be free. But since you had no shame then, it is only natural that you will be ashamed now.

The trouble is, you are too proud of yourself. You have an idea the world takes you as always hav-ing been honest, and you do not want to let them know the truth in the matter. You don't want to humble yourself. You imagine that you have exalted yourself by repentance. You imagine you stand high in the eyes of your friends. "And whosoever shall exalt himself shall be abased; and he that shall humble himself shall be exalted."—Matt. 23:12.

There is no degradation so great, so shameful as that originating from dishonesty and pride. There is no person so low down in the eyes of God as the one who has been false and dishonest, and too exalted to confess it. There is no exaltation like that originating from an honest confession and restoration. There is no honor like that originating from a willingness to correct past wrongs regardless of the cost or what men say. When you become real earnest about your salvation, when you are willing to become anything and do anything and be anything for the Lord, restitution will not be hard for you. You have no idea of the joy resulting from a knowledge of the fact that you have done what you could.

You may not be able to think of all your dishonesty the first day of your repentance. I have known men who made restitution years after their repentance. These things are not always revealed to you at once. I have known ministers of the Gospel to make restitution for things committed years before. It had not been revealed to them in such a manner before, but as fast as it was revealed, they restored. I might name like experience in my own life, but I shall not, but simply say that as fast as the Lord reveals those things to me I go to work and settle up. The devil is sharp; he tries to take advantage of people in every way possible; if nothing else will do he torments you over past dishonesty. It has been a settled fact with

me that the devil cannot get me down in that way.
I'll settle up back tracks so quickly that he does not
know what to do next. I am one of those kind who
does not want to be tormented with past wrongs
which are possible for me to correct. If it is beyond
my power to do so, I know the Lord will not hold me
responsible. It is all under the blood.

You may say that restitution is all unnecessary.
May I ask you a plain question: Is it wrong for the
evil doer to go back and correct matters? No, you
say, it is not wrong. Now I ask, if it is not wrong to
do so, what else must it be? There is only one thing
it can be, and that is, it must be right. Now if it is
right, it is your duty, and a genuinely converted soul
will not hesitate to do it.

I know that there are thousands of sinners who
refuse to come to Christ for fear of restitution. They
know if they confess Christ, these things must be revealed, and rather than do that they stay away. But
that is as good a scheme as the devil wants. If he
can keep you on those grounds he is satisfied. Do
you see how the devil works you? He made you believe when you were committing those wrongs that
you would enjoy it and gain by it. But now you see
your wrongs and instead of the comfort he promised,
he is shaming you so much that you will not repent.
Rather than lower yourself any more, the devil tells
you, "Keep it secret, don't confess such stuff as that.
You just reform now and that will do just as well.
It would be a shame for you to lower your honor
now." He is only giving you a false hope again as

he did before. Now he makes you believe that you
gain nothing in restitution. He will come to you later on when he has completely fastened you, and even
in hell torment you more than ever for not repenting
and making restitution when you had the chance and
knew it was right.

The best thing the devil has ever made of any
man yet was a perfect fool. He leads men around
making them believe that he is working for their interest when the fact is, he is making fools out of
them, subject to his ridicule and everlasting torment.
Where are you, my sinner friends? Are you ashamed
to come to Christ? Are you afraid of restitution? Is
the devil getting his work accomplished with you?

When you are converted, something else will appear. To be truly converted means to

Be Filled with the Love of God

and that means to have charity; it means to rejoice
not in iniquity, but to rejoice in the truth. Instead of
enjoying sin and untruth you now enjoy righteousness and truth. Instead of spending your precious
time in conversations of foolishness, you now enjoy
conversations of wisdom and truth. Instead of reading and feeding on dime novels, you now feed upon
the Word of God. You now enjoy moral literature
instead of light, flimsy, trashy stuff. Some of you
church members, if you were converted, would enjoy
the reading of your Bibles instead of spending the
Lord's day on Sunday newspapers. Show me a man
who makes a habit of reading newspapers on Sunday,

and I will show you a man who needs salvation. Newspapers, like all other articles, have their place; but no Christian can spend the Lord's day on them and live very long spiritually. I find entirely too many church members who say they cannot interest themselves in the Bible and wonder what is the matter. There is only one thing the matter that I have ever found, and that is, they are not converted. The converted man and woman love the truth, and God's Word is truth.

One of the greatest and possibly one of the most universal evidences of conversion is that of

FORBEARANCE

Any one can bear a few things, any one can forbear with others so long as everything goes to suit their pet ideas and fancies; but there is only one class of people who can bear all things, and that is the class who have charity. Those who are converted. Charity "beareth all things, believeth all things, hopeth all things, endureth all things." The converted soul beareth all things, not only a few; it matters not whether encouraging or discouraging, whether good report or evil. There is nothing able to separate them from the love of God. It matters not what false doctrines may be thrown before them. They are able to test it in the light of God's Word and to bear the evil influences.

The converted have learned to bear with others. Instead of continually criticising others, they are kept busy on themselves. They have no time and less yet desire to criticise others. They have learned to obey

the plain command, "Judge not that ye be not judged." One person may be on the mountain top of
Christian experience, another down in the valley of
formality, neither is able to judge the other, neither
one understands the circumstances of the other and it
is impossible for either one to pass a just judgment
upon the other. Strong, devoted Christians are criti-
cised, very often unjustly today, and I find invariably
that the critics are among the formal class who have
not enough spiritual fire about them to cause even a
spark.

Never was I disgusted so much as when I was
with a certain church member who was a professional critic. When in the home all I remember was criticism on others; on the way to church there was a
continual harangue on the dress of some of the members; on the way home, if we have a right to judge
the future by the past, the same thing is repeated with
even more emphasis. It matters not how many sinners have repented during the service, nor how spiritual and piercing the sermon was, they think of nothing but the dress of this sister or that brother. Show
me a person like that and I will show you one who
has his religion in his dress. Show me one like that
and it matters not how plain or how modest his dress
may be, and I will show you one, who if disrobed of
his clothing, would also be disrobed of his religion. I
cannot see how such people expect to get along after
the resurrection.

My dear people, what we need is a deeper experience. We dare not stop until we reach the heart. I
believe in modest apparel as seriously as any one, but

if you think you can be converted by changing your dress only, you will be badly disappointed some day. It is an inward work, a heart and a mind work. Paul tells us to be transformed by the renewing of our minds. It matters not how you may be renewed outwardly, if you are not renewed inwardly it will avail you nothing. If your mind is not changed and renewed you are not converted; and that means that you are condemned, no matter how plain your dress or how great your criticism.

There is no need of you being in darkness on this matter. If your mind is new, you will know it. If there is one thing the church today needs, it is to have a general conversion of many of her professing Christians. If there is any one thing that is killing the church, it is the cold, formal religion of many of its members. We never can expect the best results until more of our people get genuinely converted and begin to worship God in spirit and in truth. We have entirely too much dry-goods religion. Many are running away with the demon of fashion, others with the imp of formalism. May God help us to understand what it means to be converted! May we have a genuine experience whereby we may know that we are sons of God. We must have a heart work and not only a surface work. We need spiritual talkers and not grumblers. Whenever we are converted we shall bear all things without criticism or grumbling.

But I conclude with the text, "Except ye be converted and become as little children ye shall not enter the kingdom of heaven." There are only a few things

which we as a human family can universally agree upon. We differ widely in many of our conclusions,
but we have no chance to differ on Christ's simple
text today. We may and often do differ as to how
conversion is brought about, but we cannot differ as
to its necessity. We cannot deny that no conversion
means no heaven. Without climbing a ladder we
never reach the top. Without climbing the only way
to heaven you cannot expect to reach it. Unless you
are willing to take the way prepared and climb
gradually, round by round, you shall never reach the
glory world. Unless you are willing to submit, to
repent and be converted, you shall never enter the
kingdom of God.

Will you lift your eyes with me a few moments
and behold the heavens still open; the angels of God
still ascending and descending upon the Son of man;
will you behold the celestial glory of the world beyond, the purity, the happiness, and the eternity of it;
will you with the publican say, "Lord, be merciful
to me a sinner;" will you throw yourself into the
loving arms of the Savior and say, "Here Lord, convert and cleanse me, start me on my way to heaven;"
will you take Him by faith? My prayer to God is
that you may.

"The wind bloweth where it listeth, and thou hearest the sound thereof, but canst not tell whence it cometh, or whither it goeth; so is every one that is born of the Spirit."—Christ.

"Mere outward reformation differs as much from regeneration as white-washing an old rotten house differs from pulling it down and building a new one in its place."—Toplady.

The true social regenerator is the faithful preacher of the Gospel; and the only organization truly able for the regeneration and perfection of society is the Christian Church.

"The beauty of holiness has done more, and will do more, to regenerate the world and bring in everlasting righteousness than all the other agencies together."—Chalmers.

REGENERATION

"Ye must be born again."—Jno. 3:7.

Tonight we come to the fifth round of the ladder. We have Christ's own words for authority. The new birth or regeneration is a positive necessity. "Ye must be born again." There are no exceptions or reservations about it. It is a plain case at which we need not marvel.

Men are apt to think that so long as they stay away from Christ and do not confess Him they are breaking none of His commands. There is no grander way for people to deceive themselves. It is a positive necessity to be born again; it is obligatory upon every soul and so long as men refuse, they are breaking one of the most evident and necessary obligations.

Truly enough, where there is no law there is no transgression, but here is the law, "Ye must be born again." Have you been obedient, or are you still resisting? There is an awful condemnation resting upon you. The agnostic boasts in that as he says, "I do not know." Men plead ignorance of the law but that does not annihilate either the law or its penalty. That does not change the authority or the validity of the text. The obligation still remains, "Ye must be born again." Do you know it? Do you believe it? Will you accept it? Have you been born again? A proclamation from the lips of the Son of God. Have you obeyed it? How can you

dare to stand out against God? Are you not fearful? The Lord will not always bear with you.
These days of grace will come to a close.

You may say that you love God; you may think
that you are obedient and you need not specially be
born again. You may be honest in your statements.
Every infidel says that he loves God. If I should
tell them that they do not love God they would be
very seriously offended. The truth is, they do love
a god, one of their own ideals, but not the God of
the Bible. They think that they love the God of the
Bible, the God of the Christian, but any one who
knows the Bible knows very well that they do not,
and neither does the one who refuses the new birth.
You do not even know the God of the Bible. "Here-
by we do know that we know Him if we keep His
commandments."—I John 2:3. Have you kept His
commandments? Have you been born again? Unless you have been, you neither know, less yet love
the God of the Bible. And that is not all; unless
you have been obedient and unless you have been
born again, you are this very night on your way to
destruction as fast as the wheels of time and neglect
can carry you.

The Lord might have laid out another plan before Nicodemus, but He did not. I have often
wondered how it was that He laid out such a simple
and such an easy way. Why did He not make it more
difficult. Why did He not send us through hell for
about ten million centuries and then redeem us?
That would not have been too hard. We do not

deserve such an easy way. Why did he not set before us a hundred ways and tell us to choose the one that suited us best. The Lord knew His business. He knew man and He knew that it would be far better to have but one way and that without a substitute.

During the war of secession, if a man was drafted for service and was unwilling to serve, he was excused, provided he would pay sufficient money for his substitute. He had his choice; he could go himself or he could substitute if he desired. But in this case we have

No Substitute

"Ye must be born again." No exceptions or reservations are made. He does not say, if you want to, if you are ready, if you feel like it, or if you are good enough; that does not matter. Ye must be born again; ye must be regenerated; ye must be made over.

Men, and women, by the millions, are losing their souls because they are trying to substitute for the new birth. They substitute their moral works, their infidelity, their scepticism, their ignorance; their goodness and their neighbors' badness; their false modesty and humility. "My" religion and not the religion of Jesus Christ. "My" church and not the Church of the Lord Jesus Christ. Oh, that the day may come when men and women will stop this soul-destroying substitution; when they will learn that the new birth means more than form, more than "joining church," more than outward appearance.

God speed the day when not only the professional sinner may be born again but also thousands of our
cold, North-Pole church members! May they too
learn that, "Ye must be born again."

It is an undeniable fact that there are in the
visible church those who know not the first principle
of regeneration. They have their traditions, their
substitutes, and they cling to them like a leech; hanging upon a false hope, having a form of godliness
but denying the spirit and power thereof.

The days of formal worship are past. The time
of typical sacrifices is past. The time is at hand
when the true worshipper shall worship, not in this
mountain, nor in Jerusalem, but in spirit and in
truth. It is a heart, not a surface work. It is a
decoration of the heart, not of the body. It is the
destruction of a stony, wicked heart and the
creation of a new. It is a change and transformation
of mind rather than material. In fact, it is an inward and not an outward work.

I remember a few months ago in my evangelistic
experience, a fashionable young lady was convicted
of her sins and among the number who confessed
Christ at that meeting, she was one. When she returned to her home that night and her eyes fell upon
her fancy dresses, her hats and feathers, she broke
down in tears. The thought of sacrificing all these
was more than she could stand. She thought regeneration was a surface work and that Christianity
was all upon the outside and it was more than she
could stand to turn from fashions to humility and

modesty. But when she found in Romans 12:2 that it was a matter of being "Transformed by the renewing of the mind," a very different picture passed before her. She knew that without a renewed mind and heart, all of her renewing of dress would avail nothing. She learned that a renewed mind would gladly give up worldly pride and fashions. She learned that modesty was sure to follow a transformed mind. It is a spirit, an inner work and not a material and outer work. If a man is wrong outside it is because he is wrong inside. Man grows from the inside outward and not from the outside inward.

Not long ago I was in company with a party who was a member of a certain denomination and when the wearing of gold was brought up by a worldling who was also present, this party at once said, "We don't wear gold, we are ————," naming his church denomination. I was somewhat shocked at his expression. If people do not wear gold simply because they are Mennonites, Dunkards, Methodists, Baptists or any other church denomination, I would not give the snap of my thumb for all their regeneration and Christianity. If we as a church lay aside fashion and the putting on of apparel simply because we are Mennonites, we may just as well put them all on as far as our salvation is concerned.

If I know anything at all about the new birth, I put away fashion and costly apparel, not because I am a Mennonite, nor because I am a member of any other church, but because it is a plain Gosepl teaching and because I have been born again, because I am a child of God and not of the devil.

That is not all. When sinners are born again it will be a small task to leave worldly things. You need not continually keep cutting here and there, but it will be a natural result, and just as an apple ripens upon the tree and falls off, so will your worldliness. Would to God that people would get a heart religion and not some formal concern! Would that people would stop their continual substitution! "Ye must be born again."

To be born again is

NOT ALL OF CONVERSION

Sinners may be turned from their wicked ways, but if they refuse to go further they cannot be born again. As the work of conversion belongs to God so regeneration also belongs to Him. "Ye must be born again," shows clearly that there must be some outside agent at work in regeneration. Man's part is to submit. God does the work. In conversion the sinner is arrested and turned; or in other words he is torn down, but in regeneration he is made over and he becomes a new creature. These two conditions may take place almost simultaneously or it may take more time; it depends largely upon how willing the convert is to be made over or regenerated. There must be a willingness, not only to be torn down, but also to be built up again. The Lord will work just as fast as you will allow Him. There is no excuse for a half-way work. Where a soul is sincerely willing to give up, the work will be carried through to perfection. Conversion and regeneration go hand in hand and occur almost simultaneously when the applicant is willing to submit to the conditions.

Neither is

WATER BAPTISM

the new birth. Strange how people will substitute for regeneration. Many believe that putting a sinner down under the water and taking him out again is being born again. That may be one kind of birth but not the salvation kind. Not the kind which removes sin and saves the soul. If it were, it is evident there would be more saved people in the world today.

No doubt you have seen hundreds of people go down into the water. I was standing on the shore of Lake Michigan sometime ago watching some hundred and fifty boys and men bathing. I noticed many of them go down under the water cursing and swearing and they came out just the same way. Being born of water had no effect on them whatever. It should be very clear to every rational man and woman that if a man goes down into the water a sinner he will also come out a sinner, unless he should repent while under the water, and most sinners need more time than that for repentance. Further than that, if water baptism is regeneration then it would be impossible for some people to be saved. There have been, there are, and always will be times when water baptism will be impossible. It takes more than water to accomplish a new birth. "Except a man be born of water and of the Spirit he cannot enter the kingdom of God." It takes more than material to initiate into the spiritual kingdom, which is a work of Spirit and of fire.—Matt. 3:11.

My sympathies went out a short time ago for a certain Christian lady who was much concerned in the salvation of her husband and child. Day after day she plead with him to be baptized until he finally consented. At the same time she also had her infant babe baptized. Now she said she was perfectly satisfied and at ease because she knew that they both were saved. No matter what their life would be. She was substituting water baptism for regeneration. The devil is surely getting to be an expert in his business.

Notice how ridiculous it comes out. If water baptism of any kind is the means of taking away sin and regenerating a life and keeping it saved, then the life and the blood of Jesus Christ can have no place in the plan of salvation. No one who believes in Jesus Christ at all would be willing to exclude Him from the salvation plan; yet that is exactly what we do when we say that water baptism saves a soul. We take away the cleansing power of the life and blood of Christ. Why should Christ live and die if water baptism is sufficient?

How people can expect a spiritual condition to result from a material and typical cause is a mystery to me. It is contrary to spiritual law. The agent of a result must always be greater than the result itself. Neither natural water nor any other material thing can ever produce regeneration. The new birth is a spiritual condition or a spiritual result, and it cannot originate from a material or a typical cause. Water baptism is only a type, only, "The answer of a good conscience toward God."—I Peter 3:21. Only an outward manifestation of what has taken place within. It cannot, it dare not, God never intended that it should be substituted for regeneration.

Regeneration means

A New Creation

A new creature. "Therefore if any man be in Christ, he is a new creature; old things are passed away, behold all things are become new."—II Cor. 5:17. The Word says nowhere that if a man reform or change his outward appearance he shall be a new creature. It does not say that if the sinner is baptized with water he shall be a new creature. It does not say, if you join the church you shall be a new creature, but, "If a man be in Christ he is a new creature." It means a new building.

Without me telling you, you know that before you can have a new building here, you must first pull down and destroy the old one. The building cannot operate upon itself; some outside force must act upon it. You would put a number of men to work with hammers, saws, crowbars and the like, and soon the building would be down. You then would destroy the old foundation and clear it away to one side. But if some part of the building or foundation would seem to resist in coming apart, you would put a little extra force to that part and if nothing else would do, you would apply a little dynamite and blow the thing to pieces. After all is down then you begin a new building. You work in as much of the old material as possible and refuse the rest and when you are through you have a new building, a new creation.

With the new birth, it is the same. Before you can have a new buiding, a new creature, you must first allow the old one to be destroyed. You must allow the Lord to take you apart, and to take away even the foundation upon which you have been building. How much of your old talent and intellect the Lord can use in the new building depends upon its quality. But if you do as many have, resist when the Lord begins to take you apart, saying, "I can't see any use in this or that," and you refuse to submit, there are one of two things which must and will happen to you. Either the Lord will allow you to have your own way and allow you to go unregenerated, or He will apply some of His blasting powder and blow you to pieces. He may take you through the same process that he did myself. I had my idea of regeneration and thought I had the proper one. No one could change my pet views. I actually got so far with it that I felt that I was almost ready to apply for a patent on it. I refused to give in. The Lord kept working and trying to get me to pieces in order to build up a new creature, but I had an idea that I could do it myself, so I resisted. I was like an old stump, which has been struck at, chopped and split at and still stood in the way. Finally the Lord went to work in dead earnest. He drilled a hole clear to the heart of the old stump, put down a good load of blasting powder and completely raised me from off my foundation and allowed me to hang in the air for a while.

Finally when I saw what had happened, I began to look around for a safe place on which to drop. It looked dangerous. All about me were infidelity, scepticism, atheism and a whole catalogue of other devilisms 'which were opening their hungry mouths without measure. I finally came down again and as Providence would have it, I came down standing on my feet. I kept pretty quiet for a while. I looked one way a while and then another. I did not know whether I was safe or not. But the best of all I saw that I was undone and helpless; I turned and said, "Here, Lord, I am; if you can make anything of me, all right. Go ahead, for I am done."

The wonderful thing about it all was, that from that very day I was on a new foundation. I felt different. I was different. The foundation felt more durable. The Lord began to build, and He has been building continually. Day by day He adds to the regenerated soul a new story, and as we move from one to the other it is always larger and more responsible and more glorious. We learn to enjoy with the poet,

"Build thee more stately mansions, oh my soul;
    As the swift seasons roll!
Leave thy low vaulted past!
Let each new temple, nobler than the last,
Shut thee from heaven with a dome more vast;
    Till thou at length art free,
    Leaving thine outgrown shell
    By life's unresting sea!"

When the old building is once down and forsaken, then there is hope for a new one; not before. So long as you resist and refuse to be made over, you can never enjoy a new creation. We cannot tell you all that it means. We cannot tell you all that we enjoy. Words cannot express what it means for old things to pass away and all things to become new. Words cannot express the beauty of a new will, of new desires instead of old. No human tongue can utter the vast difference between the old and the new likes. With the old will nothing but sin could be enjoyed. The devil was the architect of character; he used bad timber and poor foundations. The building could not possibly stand through eternity. The old material was of immoral thoughts, words and conduct. There was no desire for anything pure and holy. The whole thing was condemned.

But when the old building, the old man, was destroyed, and a new man started, there came also

NEW DESIRES

There came desires for the work of God. A desire for the literature of God. The works of a moral and God-fearing poet have a different melody. With more appreciation than ever can we understand the "Psalm of Life." With more sympathy than ever can we read the story of "Enoch Arden." With more appreciation than ever can we take up the works of Longfellow, Tennyson and Bryant and many others and enjoy them. And above all the old Bible seems more true and more sacred than ever. Old things have passed away and all things have become new.

No time before could we understand that "The heavens declare the glory of God and the firmament showeth his handiwork." With more enjoyment and understanding than words can express we behold the works of nature. No creation so great nor none so small but we see the glories of God. Even the tiniest flower hidden away from the world reveals to us the love and wisdom of God. While we behold it with a sense of pity, yet it is rejoicing in the fact that it is fulfilling its mission in life equally as well and even more perfectly than we. Its days are only few. Its life is pleasant and sweet and encouraging to the regenerated man. As it closes its lovely eyes in death and passes away, it leaves its parting message, "My service to man is complete, I shall return from whence I came. Only a few more days, a few more years and this shall be your lot." Where is the soul that sees nothing in nature! That cannot see itself in nature! Show me that man or woman and you show me one who is unregenerated.

But finally, the newborn man never before so much enjoyed the deep things of God. The new desire is now for the spiritual world. Hour after hour we love to meditate on spiritual things. We enjoy a closer union with the infinite. We read the inspired volume time after time with renewed interest. It never grows old. The more we learn, the more we desire to learn; mountain tops along the horizon appear only to be illuminated with the rising of the Son, only to be reached when Jesus comes. From mountain top to mountain top the soul leaps in its eternal liberty. The more our eyes are open the higher we rise upon the mountain, the broader the fields appear, and the more we see that we cannot understand. The more we cannot understand the more faith we can exercise. Oh, the boundlessness, the unspeakable glories of a new soul! Surely all things have become new. Surely the old house is down and a new one erected; the old man is down, the new man is coming forth. It is only because of the new birth; only because of regeneration which the Lord has accomplished through His Spirit power and our willingness to submit. Would you have such an experience? "Ye must be born again."

I hear so many honest souls ask,

How Can We Know That We Are Born Again?

I heard a young man say only a few days ago that we cannot know, and that we must simply take chances on it. What a mistake! No man can have a more blunderous view of this question. You can know whether you are born again and you need to take no chances on it. You take your chance on games of chance, but regeneration never was and never will be a game of chance. It is a sure thing, and if you are born again you will know it more positively than you will know that you have been born naturally. Doubt is one of the devil's traps, and if he can make you doubt that you are born again, and get you discouraged, he will be more than satisfied, he has accomplished his work.

A young man said to me not long ago, "Oh, if I knew that I was saved for sure, I would be the

happiest man on earth, but how can I know that?"
I have wondered and said since, Why is it that men
will believe the devil rather than God? There are
hundreds of positive tests in God's Word that will
be sufficient to convince and satisfy any soul whether
or not he has been regenerated and is saved. If you
will read the Word you will find them. Listen to
I Jno. 5:1.

"WHOSOEVER BELIEVETH THAT JESUS IS THE CHRIST
IS BORN OF GOD"

Do you believe it? Can you say that we cannot
know whether or not we have been born of God? Can
you conscientiously and honestly call for a more
simple and more evident test? Do you believe that
Jesus is the Christ? Why do you allow doubt to arise
in your mind when you have the plain promise of
God? You are mistrusting your best friend when
you do it. Can you not follow the Savior's plan and
quote Scripture on the devil when he comes to you
with doubt? You have plenty on your side if you
will only use it. If you truly believe that Jesus is
the Christ, you have been born of God.

And what shall I say to you, my sinner friends?
First, I know that there is no doubt in your mind as
to whether or not you have been born again. You
need not ask, Am I really born again? You know
you are not. The Lord knows you are not. And
the devil knows you are not. You know you are
still on the old foundation. It is trembling with you
now; you are fearful of the old building, you are
standing alone; you feel forsaken; the devil has not

made you as strong as he had promised. You feel condemned because you do not believe in the Lord Jesus. You know that you have never been regenerated. You know that no change has ever come into your life, and that the wrath of God is awaiting you.

Our sympathies go out for you. We know by experience that life is miserable for you. We want you to be regenerated. We want you to enjoy life with us and we know that when once you shall become willing and believe that Jesus is the Christ that you shall be born of God. Will you allow the Lord to work tonight? Will you submit yourself now?

Faith in Jesus Christ is the first mark of the new birth. Faith includes more than most people want to accept. Simply consenting to the truthfulness of a fact is not faith. It requires more than simply consenting that Jesus is the Christ. It means more than simply having your name on a church book. It means believing strongly enough in the Lord that you become willing to submit to Him, take Him by faith, trust and obey Him. Until you are willing, and actually do obey Him, you have no living faith in Him.

A lack of full and unreserved faith in Jesus Christ accounts for the reason why people say that they cannot know whether or not they are saved. They have not been submissive and obedient as they should have been, and it is only a natural result for doubt to arise. If you have the least doubt, I would advise you to look up your accounts; see whether you have been as faithful as you should have been, because there is no necessity nor cause for doubt. Where there is doubt there is also reason for it. A doubtful case need not be so.

I find another evidence of the new birth.

"WHOSOEVER IS BORN OF GOD DOTH NOT COMMIT SIN

for his seed remaineth in him and he cannot sin, because he is born of God."—I Jno. 3:9. Do you yield to temptation every time that the devil comes along? Do you commit sin? If that is the case, you need not ask, Have I been born again? You need not be in doubt, because His Word is plain that if you are born of God you will not commit sin.

A certain man, who claimed to have been a Christian, said to me some time ago, "No matter how far we advance in the Christian life, we after all are bound to sin every day. It is only natural and we sin against our better knowledge and cannot avoid it." What shall I believe, the testimony of such a man or the testimony of God? Did you ever hear of men telling lies? Did you ever catch God in a lie? I think it will be wise to believe God in this matter and not man. Listen to what God says and believe God above man: "He that committeth sin is of the devil, for the devil sinneth from the beginning." "Whosoever is born of God doth not commit sin."—I John 3:9.

Show me the man or woman, be they in the church or out of it, who commits sin, and you show me one who needs to be born again. Show me the

person who lies and I will give you his nearest rela-
tive, his father; "Ye are of your father, the devil
. . . . . for he is a liar and the father of it."—Jno.
8:44. Are you guilty of any form of sin? You need
not ask, Have I been born again?

But I hear some one say that it is impossible to
go through this world of temptation without sinning
now and then. Be careful what you say. God says
that if you are born of God you do not commit sin.
Do not set yourself up against God. We will confess
this much and we know God will grant the same.
He knows man is weak and subject to mistakes. Our
High Priest, Jesus Christ, is touched with the feelings
of our infirmities (Heb. 4:15). The Lord knows
that we are weak and very much limited in our
knowledge and understanding. He knows that we
stumble, but there is a vast difference between committing sin and making mistakes resulting from human weakness. The sinner commits his sin knowingly and willfully. The child of God, by the grace of
God, does not walk voluntarily and knowingly into
sin. The seed of God is in him. Human weakness
in the devoted child of God is not sin to him. So
long as we have the seed of God in us, we cannot
sin. So long as you go on sinning every day, there
is something wrong with you. What you need is to
be born of God; to be regenerated.

We need not ask you, sinner friend, whether
or not you are free from sin. I need not ask you
whether you have sinned today. Your own confession would be, "Yes, I have sinned, and I am not

free from sin." If such be your condition, it is plain enough that you have not been born of God. If you have not been born of God it is then a fact that you are still in your sin and that brings before you the fact that, "Except ye repent ye shall all likewise perish."

Should I ask you, Have you not long desired to be free from sin, I am sure if you were honest in your reply you would say, "Yes, long have I desired to let loose and get away if I only could. I know that sin is only making me miserable and unhappy." I cannot set you free. Your friends cannot set you free. There is none but God who can deliver you. He will liberate you when you are willing. You need not leave this building tonight without being liberated, if it is your will to be free. What you need is to believe and repent, and the Lord will build you over again.

You say there is no use to try; that there is no hope for you any way. You say you cannot get loose from those cursed habits which are blasting your life, both mentally and physically. I confess with you that you cannot get loose yourself but the Lord can loose you. The Lord Jesus has power on earth to forgive sin and to deliver from the same.

Sometime ago I met a young man who was tied up in a sinful habit which he had been trying to break away from. It was killing him inch by inch, and only a little time of continuance and he would have been a physical, moral, intellectual and spiritual wreck. He saw his danger and called for help.

After a short conversation with him I said, "My dear friend, there is no hope on earth for you, only through the power of God. You may try as long as you live and you will never get loose. It takes the power of God to set you free. If you are willing to try the Lord, we will bring your case to Him for deliverance and forgiveness and I know that if you trust Him for power you will enjoy freedom."

After a short season of earnest prayer with him, he confessed that the Lord had been merciful and had forgiven him and more than that, he was sure that he was free from the sin which would shortly have ruined him. So far as I have been able to learn, he is still living a true, devoted, victorious life. There is hope for you to be set free from sin if you will trust the Lord and be born again.

I find another mark of the new birth. As a natural result of faith in Christ and liberation from sin we have a righteous life. "If ye know that he is righteous, ye know that

EVERYONE THAT DOETH RIGHTEOUSNESS

is born of him."—I Jno. 2:29. Is there any possible chance for us to be in doubt? It is perfectly clear to me. If you know your own life, whether it is righteous or unrighteous, you must know whether or not you are born again.

Righteousness means more than moral works. It means more than being a regular attendant at church. It means more than to enjoy a sermon so intensely as to go to sleep and snore over it. It means more than to drop a penny into the contribution box whenever you are compelled to. Somehow I have little sympathy for penny Christians. The only reason they have for giving a penny, I often think, is simply because they have no half-pennies. There are widows now and then who give all they have in one mite and God is just as well pleased with them as though they gave millions. But righteousness means more than so much moral works. It means to be animated for a service for humanity. To act and do because we have the love of God in our heart. Because we desire to see the world saved. Righteousness means more than can be seen or manifested in material ways. It must originate in a spiritual source.

It matters not how well you may treat yourself; how moral you may be. It matters not how good your works may be; how many dollars you may give to charity; how honest you may be in all of your business transactions. It matters not how much your friends may enjoy your kindness, unless you have been born again, all of your doings cannot count for genuine righteousness. It is all counterfeit; all self-righteousness, and the self-righteous man has no promise.

I meet men and women every day who are good moral characters so far as any one knows. No one can say one word against them as neighbors. They are the most accommodating; they are honest, honorable and sociable. They are a perfect picture of the rich young fellow who came to Christ. He was moral, had kept the law from his youth up; but

Christ said, "One thing thou lackest." He had everything except, "Come and follow me." "Now Naaman, captain of the hosts of the king of Assyria, was a great man with his master, and honorable, because by him the Lord had given deliverance to Syria; he was also a mighty man in valor, but he was a leper."—II Kings 5:1. So I find people, they are sociable, honest and honorable, but they are lepers. They are sinners. They lack something. It is hard for them to see it. They think that they are just as good as anyone else. They only judge from outward appearance, when it is an inward and not an outward condition.

Unless you have been born of God, it matters not how good your works may be or how honorable you may be in the eyes of the people, you are still a leper, a sinner, an unrighteous man. God's word explains it in no other way, and I dare not. Righteousness comes alone through the regenerated life.

It may be practically unnecessary to mention the fact that a sinner cannot claim righteousness. They feel offended when we do not allow them the credit for righteousness. But how dare we when the plain word of God does not? The sinner demands respect and expects his good qualities to be of equal value as those of the Christian. He cannot see the difference in effect of the truth told by himself and the same truth told by a righteous, regenerated man. He cannot see how the dollar given to charity by the righteous man can be of any more glory to God than the one given by himself. He sees no difference, for he looks upon the temporal appearance only. He does not understand the spiritual secret, "Without me ye can do nothing." Their works may be ever so moral and generous, but unless prompted and animated by the Lord Jesus they cannot count for righteousness. God is righteous; hence "Every one that doeth righteousness is born of Him." The devil, all will confess, is not righteous. Hence every one who is a follower of the devil cannot claim righteousness. The Bible gives no other leader for the sinner than the devil. If you would have righteousness, my dear people, ye must be born of God.

We know further that we have been born again, that we have passed from death unto life,

BECAUSE WE LOVE THE BRETHREN (I Jno. 3:14)

Any one knows whether they love the brethren. If he fails to know it it is not the fault of God but of himself. There is no excuse for doubt. The Lord does nothing in secret. It is our privilege to know what we are. We can know very well what our wishes and desires toward our fellowmen are. We know whether we wish them success or failure, God's grace or wrath. We know whether or not we desire them the same blessings as we ourselves desire. If we were left ignorant of these things, inspiration never would have said, "We know that we have passed from death unto life because we love the brethren."

The Christian church today cannot deny the fact that they are seriously lame on brotherly love. There is so much false love. There is so much, "I'll help him if I must. I'll forgive him just to have peace

in the family. I'll overlook it just because it is him."
There is entirely too much back-biting and neighborhood gossip. Too much criticism on this brother and
that sister. Too much unjust criticism and fault-finding, just because everybody does not think just as I
do. Oh, the low ebb of some men's Christianity! The
icicles that are hanging about so many people's brotherly love!

When will our Christian professing people learn
that salvation means more than continual criticism and
fault-finding! What does it matter how my neighbor
thinks? The essential things for salvation Christ has
made plain and simple and the things which he did not
mention are left to the judgment of the individual.

My neighbor is in a very different circumstance
from mine. I should know enough, in the first place,
that it is not my business to criticise and condemn him;
and in the second place, I am in no position to judge
him. He may be upon the mountain top and I down
in the valley and I cannot give him a just judgment.
When I pass judgment, it is from a very different
point of view than his. He sees things as they really
are and I see them only as they appear to be at a distance. The Lord knew his business when he told us
to, "Judge not that ye be not judged." Ninety-nine
cases out of every hundred, where we judge our brother, we pass a false and very unjust judgment. Do not
be so prone to criticise right away, because what
appears to you as a stain on your brother's life may
be only a scar which he received on some hard fought
battle-field of victory where you would have failed

and died. This world is cold enough, let us make it no colder. Love is all that makes this world fit to live in.

I do not mean that it is improper and not an act of love for us as a united Christian family to talk over our weak points and suggest as much as possible for our spiritual growth. If there is any one thing that shows that we love one another, it is the friendly coming together and confessing our faults one to another and suggesting for the benefit of each other. How much better it would be if when a brother or a sister makes a mistake and the Bible proves the mistake, that we would go to that one in the spirit of Christ, in a kind, loving, sympathetic manner and make it known to them, instead of first scattering it over the whole neighborhood. Or instead of going to them in the spirit of priesthood and a determination to criticise and to compel them to submit and confess. When I see the ungodly criticism of so many Christian professing people, I do not wonder that wives must pray for a lifetime for their husbands to be saved, and then die without seeing their prayers answered. I do not wonder that brothers, sisters and parents are standing away when all they hear is a continual harangue of nefarious criticisms. Oh, when shall we awake and learn that if this world is ever to be won for Christ it must be through love! God speed the day when we as a Christian church may give up our criticism and faultfinding and be bound together with genuine love for Christ, for the brotherhood and for lost souls.

In the ancient Greek armies there was used what

they called a phalanx. It was composed of a body of soldiers set closely together with faces and spears toward the front. This body was then chained together so completely that no man was able either to turn or leave his place. When the orders to advance were given, they all advanced. They moved together toward the same enemy, the same place, with the same motive, and when they struck the ranks of the enemy, they were sure to enter. There seemed to be no power which was able to check them because they stood together, they moved together, and were chained together.

Whenever the Christian church forms a phalanx; when they get their eyes on the same enemy; when they turn their faces and weapons toward the front; when each soldier of the cross is willing to take his place and we are chained together with the chain of everlasting love which no power can break; and when we all move forward harmoniously together toward the world and the devil, then there will be no time for faultfinding and criticism, but there will be an awful gap opened in the ranks of the enemy.

We dare not separate. We must be chained together with brotherly love. We must follow the directions of one commander. The commands are simple. They interpret themselves. A child can understand them. The essential things we are agreed upon. The Lord gives us our weapon and points out the enemy, but he expectes us to use reason and good sense in applying our weapon. You cannot use your weapon in the same manner that the brother next to you does; you are under different circumstances. You have the same command, but your degree of power and advantage is different. But with all these varied conditions and advantages it is still necessary and possible that the great chain of God's love be thrown around us. "We know that we have passed from death unto life because we love the brethren."

But for a concluding evidence of the new birth, I shall present one which to me is the greatest of all evidences. There cannot be the least shadow of a doubt, if you have this condition you are surely born again.

As a result of faith in Christ, freedom from sin, a righteous life and genuine love for others, we have a most important and everlasting victory.

"FOR WHATSOEVER IS BORN OF GOD OVERCOMETH THE WORLD"

"Who is he that overcometh the world but he that believeth that Jesus is the Son of God."—I Jno. 5 :4, 5. I say it is the greatest evidence because it includes all before mentioned and much more. It includes not only all of the Christian graces, but a complete victory over the world and the devil.

And another thing about it is, that if a soul once overcomes the world and the devil he will not need to be in doubt as to whether he has been born of God. If you overcome the world you will know it. If you get the victory over the devil you will know it. You will know it not only in theory, but in practice and experience. Talk about having war with the devil and gaining a complete victory over him and then not know it. They say, "If we only had some evidence by which 'we can know that we have overcome; if we could only know for sure that we are born again." If a victory over the devil is not enough evidence for you, I do not know where you will ever find one. If you can overcome the 'world and the devil and not know it you surely had a much easier job of it than I had. When I won the victory and Satan hung out his flag of surrender, I saw it and I knew that meant defeat for him and victory for myself. "Whatsoever is born of God overcometh the world."

And now, my weary, sin-worn friends, you need not tell me that you are tired of your sin. You need not tell me that you would gladly overcome your sinful habits, the world and the devil. I know you desire all these. I know also that you may have your desires satisfied before you leave this house tonight. Oh, you say, "It is impossible for me, I have been in sin too long and there is no hope for me. The temptations which come to me are stronger and different than those of any one who ever lived." Let me tell you of One who was tempted in all points like as you and yet without sin. I present to you Jesus who knows your mind, knows that you think that you are more severely tempted than any man. Jesus knows that your temptations are common to man. He knows how to sympathize with you, and stands ready to advise you, to receive you and to give you victory. Will you try Him?

I know that many times you have been disgusted

with yourself because of your sin, you may have possibly felt that if it were not for a terrible future you would make an end of your miserable life. You may have expressed yourself in the same way as did a young lady with whom I am acquainted. With a weary look on her face she said, "Oh, if it was not for my awful life, my miserable life; if it was not for that awful future, I would take poison tonight!" What was her trouble? Sin was getting the victory over her. The devil was getting her just to the place where he wanted her. If he can now have her murdered he will be perfectly satisfied. The devil works just that way. If he can make a sinner of you, then make you so miserable that you will give up in despair and say that there is no hope for you, or even commit suicide, he has won his point.

You say that your enemies are too many and too strong; that even if you start you cannot hold out. Listen what God has to say to you. "We know that whosoever is born of God sinneth not; but he that is begotten of God keepeth himself and that wicked one toucheth him not."—I Jno. 5:18. That wicked one, the devil, shall not touch you if you are born of God. Do not, for the sake of your lost soul, set yourself against God. There is no power on earth or in hell that is able to overthrow you, if you trust the Lord. It matters not how great your temptation, how scarlet your sin and how innumerable your enemies. There is power in the blood, there is power in the Spirit of God. There is victory for you if you will have it.

Down on one of the streets of Kansas City one night not long ago, there stood outside of the Mission Hall a hopeless, wretched-looking character. His clothes were in rags, his eyes were bloodshot, his face was scarred and dirty. Just as our meeting was ready to close the invitation was given for sinners to confess Christ. This miserable, drunken wretch raised his hand before the door and in a pitiful voice said, "Pray for me, you can't help me, only pray for me." He then staggered away from the door but in a moment he returned, entered the door and came staggering forward to the altar. Again he began his pitiful story. "I can't help myself," he said. "I am a miserable wretch, I came here from New York City, I am a sailor, I am a rough character, I am a drunken wretch. For the past two weeks I have been drunk every night. I cannot sleep. I cannot rest. There is no more hope for me. But one thing I want to say yet and that is, I was a Christian once, but I backslid and now there is no hope for my wretched soul. Something will happen to me soon. I can't stand it any longer, pray for me."

At this moment he started staggering for the door but was stopped by one of the workers. With a little persuasion, we got the poor fellow upon his knees. After a season of earnest, faithful, fervent prayer, we arose to our feet and again he spoke. But with a different testimony. "Oh, how glorious," he said, "Can it be possible that the Lord can do it?" You ask me, Was this poor fellow converted while in such a condtion? I answer, he was reclaimed.

The Lord owned him. He had paid for him once, but he ran away and was now coming home.

Yes, my friends, it is possible; the Lord can do it. He has saved more than one miserable wretched sinner like this one and I know he can save you, be you ever so sinful. If he can save a wicked, sinful soul in Kansas City, He can also save you. Will you come tonight? Will you start for heaven? Will you climb round by round until you reach eternity's shore? Come sinner, "Ye must be born again." With all the darkness that may be hanging over you, only lift your eyes and behold the heavens still open, the angels of God still ascending and descending upon the Son of man. Will you come?

"And for their sakes I sanctify myself, that they also might be sanctified through the truth."—Christ.

"Holiness is not the way to Christ, but Christ is the way to holiness."

"Blessed is the memory of those who have kept themselves unspotted from the world. Yet more blessed and more dear the memories of those who have kept themselves unspotted in the world."—Jameson.

"A holy life is not an ascetic or gloomy or solitary life, but a life regulated by divine truth and faithful in Christian duties. It is living above the world while we are still in it."—Tyron Edwards.

SANCTIFICATION

"Sanctify them through thy truth."—Jno. 17:17.

I knew some of you would feel very uneasy and begin to look for a place to crawl out when I tell you that sanctification must necessarily have its place in one round of the way from earth to heaven. I see also that some of you are just ready to shout, simply because you have heard the word sanctification. I see before me this morning two extremes. Some of you actually detest the idea of sanctification. You have no use whatever for it. Some of you think of nothing else. You read nothing else. Sanctification with you is the whole and only thing.

The reason why you refuse to accept sanctification is, first, because you are absolutely ignorant of what we mean when we speak of it. You have a very faint idea of what the Bible says on the subject. You are ignorant of what Christ said about it. All that you know is what you have heard some extremist say, plus your own prejudice and imaginations; and it goes without saying that such a conception of sanctification is worse than none.

A second reason why you refuse to accept it is because of a lot of people who claim a high degree of sanctification and yet their lives are anything but a proof of it; and because you cannot see any difference between their lives and the lives of the worst sinner, you condemn the whole subject.

I agree with you that there are people who claim sanctification who do not know its first principle. I will go even further; I know people who claim sanctification for nothing else than a cloak for a lot of sin and ungodliness. Men and women will get down about as low in sin as it is possible for a sinner to get and about the time their sin and meanness exposes them they get what they call a wonderful conversion, a wonderful experience and become holy and entirely sanctified. You never hear of one making restitution. They never clean up back tracks. They never attempt to pay up old back debts. They are now wholly sanctified (?). If the devil ever had a trap set, this is one.

For these two reasons I find people standing at swords-points on the subject. I want you all to drop those swords now for a few moments and if you will be honest and are willing to accept the truth as God and His Word reveal it to you, I am sure that you will accept sanctification. And I will also assure you that no man can successfully hide his sin under it, either. If there is sin in him and he receives sanctification, it is sure to come out.

You may ask, What is the difference between regeneration and sanctification? There is not a great difference. If you have been regenerated you will be sanctified. Faith plus repentance, plus justification, plus conversion, plus regeneration, equals sanctification. It is a final result of the preceding steps.

It may be well before we proceed further to note

SEVERAL KINDS OF SANCTIFICATION

referred to in the Sacred Volume. I find that sanctification is not limited to spiritual conditions only. In
Genesis 2:3, I find that "God blessed the seventh day
and sanctified it." I find that under the law many material things were sanctified; the tabernacle, the temple, the priests, the altars, the vessels and sacrifices
were all sanctified by human agencies. The people
were even commanded to, "Sanctify yourselves therefore and be ye holy, for I am the Lord your God."
When the Lord spoke to Isaiah and warned him not
to walk in the ways of this people but, "Sanctify the
Lord of Hosts himself; and let him be your fear, and
let him be your dread," He made Isaiah the agent of
sanctification. But none of these are the kind of
sanctification of which we shall speak this morning.
None of these are the kind referred to by Christ
when He was praying for His disciples and for those
who should, "Believe on me through their word,"
when he said, "Sanctify them through thy truth."

The Lord knew that all the sanctifying of material things; the temple, the vessels and the priests,
would never answer for redemption. It requires a
sanctification which will reveal the guilty heart and not
conceal it. A sanctification which does not make people foolish and ridiculous, but one which is accomplished by God Himself; one that operates upon the
heart and life of man; one which will lead men to accept the whole truth and not become extremists.

In the accomplishment of this condition, the
Lord Jesus appeals to God; to the One who knows

the soul, the heart and thoughts of men. He appeals
earnestly, even at the cost of his own life, to the Creator to sanctify His followers and to sanctify them
through His own way, His own truth, His own Word.
What a wonderful and most important work it must
be if the God of heaven and earth is the only one who
is able and authorized to perform it? How anxiously then should every believing child of God lay aside
his preconceived ideas and willingly and gladly submit; come boldly to the throne of grace and allow the
Lord God to accomplish the work.

Before going further, allow me to hang out

A Danger Signal

While I do not believe that there is a possibility for
man to become too nearly like Jesus Christ; while I
do not believe that the Lord ever overdoes His work,
yet I know people who, when they get started on this
subject, never know when or where to stop. They
get wild, and forget that they are still human and
ought to remain under the care of the Lord. They
take up sanctification and run away with it.

No doubt you have fed a flock of chickens more
than once. Do you remember that greedy hen which
always came running up and would grab on to a piece
of food and at once turn and run away from the flock
and when away, as she thought at a safe distance she
began to eat. The rest of the flock were enjoying
themselves with a great many different things. The
greedy hen keeps picking at the piece which she pick-
ed on, and finally gets disgusted with it and leaves the
whole thing and either comes running back or starts

out some other direction. When I see people run away on the question of sanctification and keep picking away on it and nothing else, I must always think of the greedy hen.

The danger sign which I want to hang out is this. Do not get an idea that sanctification is the only thing which the Sacred Volume obligates us to. Do not make the blunder that many are making and sit down and read nothing and talk nothing but sanctification. Do not think that if you claim sanctification that that will answer for repentance, for conversion or restitution. Don't think that claiming sanctification will excuse you from paying your honest debts. Do not get an idea that you can have one dollar without having one hundred cents. Do not throw yourself away and become indolent and reckless and call that sanctification. On the other hand, do not expose your ignorance and your prejudice by refusing to accept sanctification at all; by refusing to admit that it is one of the most evident, one of the simplest and most necessary conditions for salvation.

Allow me to say, because I have a perfect right to do so, that we have no longer need of sanctifying the priests, the vessels, the altars, or any person or material thing in the original way. We may, and it is our duty and privilege to sanctify the Lord God in our hearts and lives as He advised Isaiah to sanctify the Lord of Hosts himself. When we admit this kind of sanctification, we mean that you give a special place in your heart and life to the Lord; that you regard and fear the Lord and not man. Sanctify the

Lord himself, and this you cannot do until He sanctifies you through His truth.

But now as to the salvation kind of sanctification. There is but one kind, and God alone, with your consent, operates that. The word in the original means to

MAKE HOLY, TO HALLOW, TO SET APART

I can now understand what is meant by the text, "If we confess our sins he is faithful and just to forgive us our sins and to cleanse us from all unrighteousness," I Jno. 1:9. I find a cleansing from all unrighteousness; a cleaning up of a filthy life. It is the working of God through His Word and through the blood of Christ by which sinners are made clean from their filth and pollution. They are not only forgiven but also cleansed from all their unrighteousness; they are made holy; they are hallowed; they are separated from sin and the world.

I find men who claim sanctification and holiness, and at the same time indulge in habits that are a shame even for the vilest sinner. I find them polluted from heart to surface; from head to foot with tobacco juice. I fail to see the cleansed part of that kind of a person. Will you please explain how a man can claim to be cleansed from all filthiness of the flesh, to be sanctified, and then indulge in this filthy, unsanitary habit which costs Christian America $750,000,000 every year and at the same time gives only $7,500,000 to Christianize the heathen?

You say you cannot see anything filthy about to-

bacco. Listen one moment. The average tobacco
chewer spits twice every five minutes; which means
about forty-five gallons per year; or in a life time of
fifty years would equal about seventy-two barrels or a
large cistern full. Or when weighed up, he spits
away three hundred and sixty pounds in a year, or in
a lifetime would equal nine tons—more than his own
weight every six months. Do you wonder why men
and boys look sickly, weak and haggard when they
spit themselves away at such a fearful rate? Dare
you say again that you cannot see that it is a filthy,
unsanitary habit?

I have it from good authority that vultures will
not feed upon dead bodies of men who have been us-
ing tobacco. The body has become so filthy and polluted that they avoid it. But now here comes the one
puzzling thing to me, and I know you ladies will sympathize with me and help me out. I am glad to see by
the expression upon your faces that you will, and will
do so gladly. Will you please tell me how it is that
you can enjoy and satisfy yourself in the company of,
and even go further and seal a life promise with a
young man whom the crows and turkey-buzzards refuse because of filthiness? Now I think you will sympathize with me in my inability to see the point; but
you explain to me and I will promise not to ask you
again.

Oh, the filthiness! I have no use for a sanctification which allows it. I fail to see the cleansing. If
there is an unclean man on earth, it is the one who
will sit around the heating stove on a cold day and
spit his filthy tobacco juice all over the stove and floor

and then expect his wife to come after him and clean up for the next time.

I cannot believe for one moment that our Redeemer while pleading with the Father to sanctify his followers ever intended that men and women should be bound to any filthy habit. I do not believe that He ever intended that when a soul was sanctified that it should be tied to a filthy plug of tobacco or a beer-glass, nor hard cider, if you please. I say I do not believe, I will make it stronger, I know and you know that the Lord Jesus gave His life to deliver men from these filthy habits. I know further that when men and women claim sanctification and at the same time cling to such filthy habits either moderately or immoderately that they are putting to shame the purity and sanctity of Jesus Christ.

Sanctification means to be cleansed from all filthiness. When God sanctifies a soul, it will be pure and clean. There is no excuse for one filthy habit. The Lord does his work well and complete. What do you suppose the pure, loving Savior thinks of your unclean life? Could you feel real comfortable sitting by His side? Could you offer to Him your old pipe and ask Him to have a smoke with you? Imagine Christ walking up the streets toward the temple in Jerusalem, smoking a cigar and now and then brushing the ashes off with his little finger! Could you draw from your pocket a plug of tobacco and offer him a chew? Oh, you filthy man! What you need is a hot scald in the cleansing spirit of God. You need your mouth and heart scrubbed out with something stronger than

Lewis Lye. You need the purifying Spirit of Jesus Christ.

"Repentant I wandered a prodigal child,
  Unclean amid sorrow and shame;
But room was not left for the sin that defiled
  My soul, when the Comforter came."

When our Savior prayed for our sanctification, He meant that we should be set

Free from the Power of Sin

"Oh, wretched man that I am; who shall deliver me from the body of this death? I thank God, through Jesus Christ our Lord." Have you been delivered from the power of sin? You may have repented and been forgiven, but are you still chained to a dead body? Have you been delivered from all evil habits whether secret or public?

When Lazarus came forth from the grave, the Savior said to those standing by, "Loose him and let him go." Take from him the grave clothes, set him free indeed. He was animated and delivered from death but was still bound hand and foot with grave clothes. Has your soul been called forth to life but still not perfectly free from the grave clothes? Are you yet bound up in sin? Are you bound to habits? Are you bound to business? Are you bound to sinful associations? Have you been delivered? Sanctification means to be loose from the power of sin.

I find people along my evangelistic path who claim that it is impossible to be free from the power of sin. There is one of two things the matter with those people; either they do not know their Bibles or they use this argument as a license for their sin. If it

is a fact that it is impossible for man to be delivered
from the power of sin then the redemption work of
Jesus Christ has been in vain and a failure. He was
sent, "To bind up the broken hearted, to proclaim liberty to the captives, and the opening of the prison to
them that are bound."—Isa. 61:1. We dare not deny
the fact that when the redemption plan has been complied with, the soul will be delivered from the power
of sin. "There is therefore NOW no condemnation
to them which are in Christ Jesus."—Rom. 8:1. "Sin
hath NO MORE DOMINION over us." If Paul's
words mean anything, they mean that it is possible to
be free from the power and condemnation of sin right
now.

Sanctification

DOES NOT REMOVE THE POSSIBILITY OF TEMPTATION

as some would have it. I have no reason to doubt the
purity and perfection of Adam before his fall. I have
evidence that the Lord created him pure and holy and
without sin, and yet he was subject to temptations. I
do not doubt God in the least that the angels were
created a little above man and as such they must be
pure and holy, and yet some of them have sinned and
fallen. I need not tell you that our Savior who utter-
ed the words of our text this morning was pure and
holy; and in Him was no guile, and yet immediately
after His baptism He was subject to temptation in
every point. Is it possible that people are so extreme on
this subject as to teach that sanctification removes all
possibility of temptation? Can you say that because
men are tempted that therefore they are not sancti-

fied? Are you more holy than Adam before the fall? Are you more holy than the angels? Are you more perfect and more pure than the Redeemer? Unless you are, you dare not claim to be in a condition where temptation is utterly impossible.

To be hallowed or to be made holy never means to be free from temptation in this life. God knows that it is more glorious for a soul to be subject to temptation and gain the victory, than otherwise, or He never would have allowed it. A tried man is of more value and a greater glory than any other, provided he can stand the trial. I would rather be a victorious soul over sin in this world than to be an angel without temptation. "Sanctify them through thy truth," means power over sin, but does not mean freedom from temptation.

NEITHER DOES SANCTIFICATION MEAN TO BECOME INFALLIBLE

It does not mean that we shall be in an absolute, divine perfection like God. How can humanity be so blinded to the truth! Some refusing entirely, while others run wild. It is because of ignorance and invariably it is wilful ignorance, because men love darkness rather than light. God "remembereth that we are dust." He knows, and we have the privilege of knowing, that we are still human and subject to human weakness. It should be clear to every mind that any man who is still wrapped up in human weakness cannot be infallible. When a man becomes infallible, he is equal with God in perfection. That can never be in this life. We need the grace and power of God every moment of our lives to keep us. We are dependent and not independent creatures. We have all sinned and come short of the glory of God. We have been deprived of our intended and original purity; it is only through the merits of the divine purity of the Son of God that we are accepted as perfect. The disease of sin is in the world and every man has been exposed and affected. Some have been healed and others have died. Even the healed yet bear the marks of sin, which renders them unable to obtain in this life absolute divine perfection.

The old sore may be healed, no pain may be felt, but the truth remains that sin has depraved us, and what has been done cannot be undone. Where the breechy brute has gone through the fence once she invariably will go through again. The Lord may clean up your life; He may repair the waste places and mend the broken links, but Satan keeps his eye upon those places, and before you are aware of it, he is at work again trying to make inroads. You may be ever so true to God; may be devoted and earnest; may be separate from the world; you may have power over sin; God may be well pleased with you: you may be perfect and before you are conscious of the fact, through your short-sightedness, you have stumbled and exposed your human weakness. You then confess, "I see my mistake; I see where I might have done better." Is there a human being, be he saint or sinner, who has no such experience? No! Such a person cannot be found. Let us not forget that we are only human, and that to be sanctified does not mean to be like God, not to be infallible.

But do not be discouraged now because of your mistakes. Sanctification does not mean to be free from human weaknesses. If it were not for our weaknesses where would the grace of God have a place? When I examine a stalk of corn which has grown a few inches high, I find within that small, green plant a perfect tassel and a perfect ear of corn. When all is laid out before my eyes, I see all that is necessary for a stalk of corn twelve feet high. It is perfect, though it has only peeped through the ground. It is not done growing. It grows every day. It is dependent every day upon the sunshine, upon the air, and upon the salts of the earth. It is entirely dependent, yet perfect every day. So it is with the genuine perfect and sanctified person. You may be very small, you may only be peeping through the surface. You lack much of being full grown. You are not at all what you hope to be. At the same time, when I analyze you, I find within you a perfect will, a perfect desire, and a perfect heart. You are not done growing. You are growing daily. You are dependent upon God, upon His love, upon His grace and upon His power. You now and then must shed a leaf, but that only gives room for a larger and a stronger one. You are a dependent creature. "Without me ye can do nothing."

Do you understand what I mean? In short it is this. You must be sanctified, but that does not mean no more chance for improvement or becoming more like Christ. You must grow; you must change every day to something better, to something nobler and something more divine. Do not make the ridiculous mistake that many do and claim that you are infallible; that you never make any more mistakes; for when you claim that, you claim equality with God, and you know that cannot be, neither is it according to His Word.

Christ never meant that through sanctification man would be brought back to Adamic or angelic perfection. I find people occasionally who almost set me down for a heretic when I present this fact. With a little thought, it is most evident that man in this life will never attain to the state from which Adam fell; nor will he attain to angelic perfection.

My dear people, if that has been your view of sanctification, if you are expecting Adamic perfection, I invite you to investigate the subject again, and allow the Holy Spirit to teach you, and you will soon get a different view of the matter. Never in this life can we gain the condition which we have lost through sin. Never in this life can we enjoy the pure, fresh and unadulterated air of God's divine love and peace in the Garden of Eden. We have lost that; we have come short. Never in this life will we enjoy a condition free from the marks and effects of sin. We have fallen from our original purity; we were perfect and holy and without one mark of sin, but we have voluntarily destroyed that condition. We have fallen, never in this world to rise so high again. The old adage is true that, "The bird with the broken pinion never soared as high again." We have broken down under sin, and though we be sanctified, that does not take us back to the original Adamic or angelic perfection. Sin has entered the human makeup and its effects cannot be fully destroyed until soul and body separate, until this mortal shall put on immortality and this corruption put on incorruption; then, and not until then, shall we understand the purity and perfection which man had originally enjoyed. Then it will be truly said that we are, "Like him, for we shall see him as he is."

But I hear some honest soul say, "If such be the case, how can man be acceptable unto God in this life? Where is our hope of salvation? What then is the use of sanctification?" "Come now, and let us reason together, saith the Lord: though your sins be as scarlet, they shall be white as snow; though they be red like crimson, they shall be as wool."—Isa. 1:18. The Lord always has a way. "Man's extremity is God's opportunity." I am glad to see people get to the place where they cry out, "What shall I do; I am full of sin; I have fallen; where is there any hope?" I am glad that I came to the same place. I was compelled to admit that I was a sinner; I did not know what to do. I tried to reform, but that did not satisfy the highest demands of my soul. I finally said, "What shall I do?" When I could do no more, then the Lord began. This text from the first chapter of Isaiah came to me. I thought of my sins, scarlet and crimson. I asked myself, "Is it possible, will He make them white as snow, will that make me just the same as though I had never sinned? No, not just the same. I have sinned. But my sins so far as they are concerned, they will be made white as snow".

But with all this, I did not regain all that was lost through the fall, but I did gain something which placed me in a condition where the Lord was willing to receive me the same as though I was as pure and as perfect as an angel. It was the Lord's plan and not mine. I cannot explain why; but I do see the love of God infinitely more in this that He makes it possible for us to be received and accepted in our depraved condition, than if we were actually able to attain to our original condition. While we must give up the hope of ever in this life gaining what we have lost, yet it is a glorious blessing and privilege which we have of being cleansed from the pollution and filth and degradation of sin. We may hold an everlasting power over sin and the devil. We can be delivered from the curse of sin and a broken law. All this we have through the answer of our Redeemer's prayer, "Sanctify them through thy truth." We do not claim and we do not desire to be entirely free from temptation in this life. Our Savior was tempted and He was the purest of all men. We cannot claim purity and holiness equal to that of God, but we do claim a perfection, a holiness and a santification which will land us finally above the ladder on the eternal, golden shore.

It is our privilege and our Savior's plan that we be separate from the world, and that we be

Appointed to a Special, Divine and Holy Service

And here is the fundamental principle of sanctification. When the Lord blessed the seventh day and sanctified it, He meant to separate that day for something special. That day was to serve a special purpose, different from any other day. He hallowed it. He made it holy. True enough, the same sun arose and set on that day. The same lovely flowers sent up their fragrance. The same birds were heard chirping and singing among the leafy branches. The same air caused a music among the twigs and leaves. The same evening twilight calmed the air, the birds, and overshadowed the landscape. All nature was at her usual place, but the day itself was sanctified. It was set apart for special service.

When our Lord prayed, "Sanctify them through thy truth," He meant separate them from the world. Let the ordinary affairs of the world go on, but let them be set apart for a divine and holy pupose; not only for one day out of seven but for every day of their lives. Let their lives be one continual praise and glory to God.

When you throw away sanctification, you are refusing the sum total of all the Christian graces and the salvation plan. There is nothing so sacred; nothing so useful; nothing so illuminating, so pure and so sweet as the life set apart from the world; set apart for divine service; one which is free from the power of sin; one which has been sanctified through the Word of God. Will you accept this condition as one step from earth to heaven?

It is so pure and so important and necessary that I often wonder whether or not the angels may tremble when touching this round. I have wondered whether or not this may be one of the most pleasant spots for them. I can better see why, "Hereafter ye shall see the heaven open and the angels of God ascending and descending upon the Son of Man." Oh, the purity of that upward way! Have you been cleansed from all filthiness? You never can pass this round until you are. You will never pass it with an impure heart, with impure habits. You and God for it, but it is my sincere opinion that you are running a terrible risk on your soul if you try to pass this round with tobacco in your mouth and beer in your stomach. God speed the hour when people will realize that before they may reach the top round of this heavenly way that they must be pure in thought, in word and in action! May the cleansing power of God take hold upon every one and make us pure, so that when He shall appear we may be like Him.

I hear an honest soul inquire,

"How is it Possible for Me to Attain to Such a Condition

What does it cost?" Some one says, it costs you nothing. If I may speak from my own experience, I must say that it cost me everything I had; it cost me my life. The reason why so many people do not have it, is because they are not willing to pay the price. All may have it, none are so destitute but they are able to give all they have. I feel safe in the assertion that you never will reach this round or this condition until you are willing, and actually do give everything in your possession.

When I say that it cost me my life, I mean that I was compelled to surrender my will to the will of

God. I was compelled to sacrifice my plans and simply say, "Here I am, Lord, use me and make of me what you want." And when I gave up to such an extent, the work was done. That is how it cost me my life. I let loose of my own plans and my own ways and took the Lord's. That is what you must do if you ever expect to gain this condition.

At the close of a meeting one night when the invitation was given for sinners to confess Christ, I was somewhat surprised to see a certain sister come forward who had been a member of the church for several years. I asked her concerning her trouble. She replied that she had confessed Christ long before, and with tears running from her eyes, she confessed that she had never been converted. I inquired a little further as to why such was her condition, and she finally confessed that it was simply because she was unwilling to surrender all. "Well," I said, "Poor soul, I cannot help you. The Lord cannot help you, unless you are willing to give up all." A surrendered will is the price of power and happiness.

It is a sad but truthful fact that I find many people in the same condition. They go so far but no farther. The first requisite for sanctification is a surrendered will; a surrendered life. When you have done this the Lord will sanctify you through His truth. Then the Savior's prayer will be answered. This condition of separation, of cleansing and sanctifying, is not for those who want it; not for those who feel like it; not for those who are ready; but for the "whosoever will." Are you willing?

"I'll go where you want me to go, dear Lord,
　　Over mountain, or plain or sea;
I'll say what you want me to say, dear Lord,
　　I'll be what you want me to be."

When you are willing, the work is continued by

GOD THE FATHER

Jude writes, "To them that are sanctified by God the
Father and preserved in Jesus Christ." It is a work
too sacred and too important to be entrusted to man.
It requires more than human power. The salvation
of an immortal soul depends upon it. A life scarred
with sin cannot cleanse itself. A soul which has been
led captive and bound in the prison of nefarious
habits cannot deliver itself. A soul which has wandered far into the dark valley of death cannot illuminate
its own path. The sinner who has started down
over the falls of eternal death and destruction cannot
rescue himself. No friend can save him. No preacher can purify him. No man, no power save God
alone can cleanse and sanctify him. No man has a
cleansing strong enough; no fire strong enough to
separate the gold from the dross. It requires a
baptism of the Holy Ghost and of fire. When this
has been acomplished, you may rest assured that you
will know it, and more than that, the world will know
it.

The work is further effected.

THROUGH THE ATONEMENT OF CHRIST

"By the which will we are sanctified through the offering of the body of Jesus Christ once for all."—Heb.
10:10. "For it is not possible that the blood of bulls

and of goats should take away sins."—Heb. 10:4. There may be a mystery, and an apparent contradiction, for some of you, in the quotation. But when studied carefully, it becomes very clear.

Under the law the blood of animals was shed for the sins of the people. They were commanded that through this their sins would be atoned for and forgiven. Not through so much blood alone were they forgiven; for, "Every priest standeth daily administering and offering oftentimes the same sacrifices which can never take away sins."—Heb. 10:11. But though faith in what the blood typified; this blood was only typical. It was only a foreshadowing of the blood and sacrifice of Jesus Christ, the reality. It was through faith in the reality and not the type, that saved the people under the law.

Now when the reality, Jesus Christ, was come, He came not to do His own will, but the will of the Father. "He taketh away the first that He may establish the second." The shedding of animal blood is only typical. It is not sufficient. It must be taken away and the reality, the life, the work and the blood of Christ must take its place. The old offerings must be taken away, and the new must be established. For this reason He taketh away the first in order that He may establish the second. We now have the reality and the atonement complete. Through the offering of the body of Christ we are sanctified.

The universalist says because Christ died once for all, therefore all will be saved. Let us say one word to you. We give you credit for believing that

Christ died once for all. We give you credit for saying that heaven is free for all, and that salvation is for all; we give you credit for all this, provided you add the Gospel proviso—that salvation and heaven is for all and all will be saved on condition that they accept the conditions. We do not deny that God wants all men saved. He wants all men in heaven. He has invited all; but we do deny upon the authority of God's Word and good common sense that a man will ever gain all this without accepting the proposed plan and invitation. "He that believeth on Him is not condemned; but he that believeth not is condemned already, because he hath not believed on the name of the only begotten Son of God." "He that believeth on the Son hath everlasting life; and he that believeth not on the Son shall not see life; but the wrath of God abideth on him."—Jno. 3:18, 36.

It may be needless for me to repeat that if a man refuses an invitation to dinner that he will get no good from the dinner. No man will go after him and compel him to come, pry his jaws open and force the dinner down his throat. If he refuses the invitation, he loses the dinner. But at the same time you claim salvation; you claim heaven and refuse the invitation and refuse the whole plan. You comfort yourself because Christ was offered, "Once for all," and so He was; in this sense that He has died never to die again; "once for all," because the work is finished for all men and to such an extent that no man or no power can improve it. But even this wonderful plan will do you no good unless you accept it. You say you do accept Him. I want to ask you, why then do you not obey Him, confess Him, learn of Him, quit your sinful habits, allow Him to clean up your sinful heart? Why do you not come to the feast? Why do you deny Christ and condemn the sacred Volume by saying that there is no punishment nor hell for the wicked?

If you will be delivered from your evil ways, if you expect any good from the offering of Jesus Christ, if you want heaven, if you will have it, you must accept His atonement. That means action. It means submission and it means sanctification.

I find another powerful agent through which sanctification is effected. In the 15th chapter of his letter to the Romans and the 16th verse, Paul speaks of being

"Sanctified by the Holy Ghost"

Allow me to drop another caution here. I wish it were untrue, but I find people who claim to be filled with the Holy Ghost who in fact know very little about Him. There is an erroneous idea abroad concerning the reception of the Holy Ghost and His power.

May I refer you once again to an experience which came under my own observation. I prefer that kind because I know they are true and actual occurrences. While preaching at a certain place, I was very much amused and yet felt sorry for a certain sister who claimed an extra supply of Holy Ghost power. She could hardly wait until the sermon began that evening. I was a little afraid something would happen that night. I saw that the congrega-

was almost as much interested in her as they were in the preacher. So I decided to put the thing to a test, and if I could get several good hearty amens out of her, then I would have more confidence in her claims.

I chose my text that evening from Joshua 7:13. "There is an accursed thing in the midst of thee, O Israel!" When I announced my text I heard a groan from her corner which I supposed was meant for, Amen. I said very little about Holy Ghost power but dealt upon secret sin, the hiding away of sin, the refusal of Christian professors to make restitution and the final result of such living.

According to my own expectation, I heard very few, "Amens" and what I did hear sounded as though they had just been forced out from beneath a lot of hidden sin. She left the meeting that night without my notice. I saw no more of her after that. I have often wondered what she has done with her Holy Ghost power.

Another mistaken idea is here; people have an idea that they must go through some awful stew for days, months and even years before they can receive the Holy Ghost. They refuse to trust the promises of God that when they ask anything in faith believing they shall have it. They are waiting for some terrible knock-down experience. They do not recognize the fact that it is a work of the "still small voice." It is quietness and harmony and not noise and discord. The Holy Ghost does not strike a man the same as lightning strikes a tree. It has no such effect.

Never was I so disgusted as while attending a certain meeting several years ago. When I saw mothers there who claimed such an amount of Holy Ghost power that they were compelled to drop from their arms to the ground helpless children while they were dancing and screaming around in the tent. I came to the conclusion that if that was the work of the Holy Ghost, I had all I cared for. I cannot blame some sinners very much when they stand away from Christ, away from the Church and away from sanctification, when they have such examples set before them. When shall people learn to read God's Word? When will they learn that the Holy Spirit works in a quiet, orderly way, and that He exposes sin instead of covering it? He tempers and controls a life decently and in order. When will they learn that sanctification and holiness originates from the Holy Spirit and are necessary for salvation?

But as a conclusive agent of this purified condition, I find it summed up in our Savior's prayer. There is one word which will include all I have said on agents of sanctification. "Thy word is truth." It is

THROUGH THE WORD OF GOD

that we are sanctified. It is through His Word that we gain submission, that we gain the Lord, that we gain the atonement of Christ and that we gain the Holy Ghost.

The infidel tells me that God—his god, cannot put his will in human language. That all goes without his telling, but the God of the Christian, the God of the Bible can put His will into any form, whether word, script or spirit. The god of Tom Paine and his deluded followers surely must be a poor stick of a thing; not able to do as much as a six-year-old school boy. The God of all creation has power and has exercised that power in putting His will down in human language; not for His own benefit, but for the benefit of humanity. "Thy word is truth." Through it we are sanctified. That means that we must go through the Word. We cannot be sanctified and at the same time know nothing about it. If you know the truth and obey it, you shall be made free.

From my own observation the Word of God receives worse treatment from the hands and tongues of men than any other book. I stop and ask a professor in English Literature what he thinks of Shakespeare's play, Hamlet. He begins to scratch his head and say, "Well, in fact, I hardly know. I have read that play a thousand times or more. I have read all of the authentic writings concerning it; I have listened to many a lecture on it; I have given it special study for thirty years but really I have come to no conclusion yet. I hardly know what to say about it; It is beyond doubt a masterpiece of literature." Well, I say, what do you think about the Bible? "Oh," he replies, "I have concluded long ago that the Bible is only a myth. It has been gotten up by some religious monstrosities who were neither sane nor intelligent." I asked him how often he has read it through. "Well, I cannot say that I have ever read it through, but I have heard lots about it." I ask him how much time he has put on it to prove its authenticity. How much he has read in favor of it. "Well, I have not used any special effort to prove it, neither have I read much in its favor, but I have heard lots." Well, how many lectures have you attended which gave a fair exposition of it? "Well, I cannot say that I have ever attended any special lectures on its exposition, but I have heard it talked about a good bit." Well, I conclude, how it is any way that you must study for thirty years, look up authorities, attend lectures, on a short human get-up like Hamlet, and then not be able to give your opinion or conclusion, and at the same time when I ask you your opinion on God's Word which was at least fifteen hundred years in being written, with sixty-six books, one thousand one hundred and eighty-nine chapters, thirty-one thousand and ninety-three verses, seven hundred seventy-three thousand six hundred and ninety-two words, and three million five hundred and eighty-six thousand four hundred and eighty-nine letters. A work which has never been equaled in poetry, in music, in prose, in oratory, in history, and in tragedy; one which shall never fail, at once, without reading it, without investigation of its authenticity, condemn it as only a myth gotten up by some crazy religious monstrosity?

You smile at the foolishness of such inconsistency on the part of intelligent men. But I find hundreds of people who do that very thing. Not in just so many words but the conclusion of their stand amounts to the same thing; and it is found not alone among the

intellectual lumps.   There is nothing that will so
quickly expose the lunk-headedness of a man as will
his condemnation of God's word, and especially if he
has never investigated it .

Possibly you say, that, "If I investigate and then
do not believe, that will excuse me." I will assure you
this, that if you honestly and sincerely investigate you
will believe. "Thy word is truth." "The entrance of
thy word giveth light." And the reason that this
world is full of infidels and unbelievers is because they
do not know God's word. They do not want to know
it; they refuse to read it. They refuse to listen; they
refuse to pray, because they love darkness better than
light. They will believe ten thousand lies about the
Bible before they will believe one truth. The old pro-
verb is surely true that, "Falsehood will travel miles
while truth is drawing on its boots." "Thy word is
truth." If men are not saved, not purified and sanctified through the word, it is because they wilfully and
stubbornly shut their eyes to the truth. If you are determined to stab out your own eyes, do not complain if
you fail to see the midday sun.

"Thy word is truth." It is plain, and if you will
read God's word instead of allowing it to lie around
on the shelf until the dust settles upon it so deep that
you can write your condemnation upon it with the
end of your thumb, you will see the truth. If you treat
God's word with half as much respect as you do your
abominable Sunday magazines and newspapers you will
be free and separate from the world of sin and evil
habits. Do not complain, my sinner friends, if you come

before the great Judge and are not cleansed. "Thy word is truth." Through it the work is done.

Permit me before I close to give a few reasons for presenting sanctification as

One Necessary Step to Heaven

I find both the Law and the Gospel full of the subject. There is no subject in the whole plan which is referred to with greater stress and which is of more importance. Even before the Savior offered his intercessory prayer, He gave to His followers the plain command, "Be ye perfect even as your father in heaven is perfect."

We need not question whether or not this command is obligatory. He refers not to Adamic or angelic perfection, but the perfection of the will, the desire and the heart.

Peter again reminded us, "Because it is written, be ye holy for I am holy." "Follow peace with all men, and holiness, without which no man shall see the Lord."—Heb. 12:14.

Hundreds of similar quotations may be given. If we had but one, it would be sufficient reason for claiming sanctification. But the fact that there are many gives no hope for excuse to any one. The simple fact that our Savior used His precious moments in praying thus for His followers should be sufficient.

Possibly you say, "Though it is a command yet it is not so obligatory as some others." You say that we ought to spend more time on other commandments which are more evident. In the first place, there is none which are more evident than this one, and in the second place you may be keeping the whole law, you may keep all the rest of the commandments, but what will you do with this declaration? "For whosoever shall keep the whole law and yet offend in one point, he is guilty of all."—James 2:10. If you want to be guilty of transgressing God's Word from cover to cover, just offend in one point; just refuse sanctification and holiness. If you want to miss seeing the Lord, just refuse to be holy. It requires purity to behold the divine. To be holy is to be pure; it is to be hallowed; it is to be able to behold the divine. "But now being made free from sin and become servants to God, ye have your fruits unto holiness and the end everlasting life." Where can mortal or divine tongue find words to make it more clear?

But my mind again is drawn to that beautiful night scene with the patriarch of old. How I would have enjoyed to spend the night in that place! But only with the mind's eye may we behold it. It seems it was too sacred ever to be repeated before sinful men. I do not wonder that it is so when I behold the open heaven and a ladder standing upon the earth and the top reaching the heavens, when the angels of God were ascending and descending upon it; and Jacob slumbering at its very foot and making no effort to ascend. Why should the Lord thus repeat Himself before such a slumbering, ungrateful humanity?

The old scene is past, never to be repeated. But I see a more beautiful way than that. "Hereafter ye shall see the heavens open and the angels of God ascending and descending upon the Son of Man." The type has passed away, and the reality is come. The way is pure and holy, or angels would never pass that way. Have you never wondered how it was that God will allow fallen man to enjoy the blessing of this sacred, angelic way? But for man and not angels has it been prepared. We may enter and march with the angels, provided we leave behind all sin and pollution; if we will be made pure and holy. We need not wait until the death hour but even now we may sing,

> "Smiling angels now surround me,
> Troops resplendent fill the skies,
> Glory shining all around me,
> While my happy spirit flies."

My fellow-pilgrims to the new Jerusalem, I appeal to you first. Have you been cleansed? Have you reached this step? Have you refused to be made pure and holy? You are losing the greatest blessing to be enjoyed on the earth. Will you make a complete surrender? Will you allow the Lord to do His most desired work? Only submit to God and believe.

And you, my sinner friends, what shall I say to you? In your countenances I see the marks of sin. You would gladly rejoice with us. You have refused Christ many times. Will you refuse Him again this morning? Would you accompany the angels, or do you prefer the devil? Will you come by the prepared way, the way which leads to life everlasting? My sincere desire and prayer is that God may sanctify you through His truth.

"There is a way that seemeth right unto a man but the end thereof are the ways of death."—Solomon.

"And an highway shall be there and a way, and it shall be called the way of holiness; the unclean shall not pass over it; but it shall be for those: The wayfaring men, though fools, shall not err therein."—Isaiah.

"In His life, Christ is an example, showing us how to live; in His death, He is a sacrifice, satisfying for our sins; in His resurrection, a conqueror; in His ascension, a king; in His intercession, a high priest."—Luther.

"Men who neglect Christ, and try to win heaven through moralities, are like sailors at sea in a storm, who pull, some at the bowsprit and some at the mainmast, but never touch the helm."—Beecher.

THE ROYAL WAY

"I am the way."—Jno. 14:6.

The Son of God proclaimed it. He has been over the road from earth to heaven, and surely knows the way. It does seem strange that men should for one moment satisfy themselves in trying to deny the way. Why should we, fallen men, set ourselves against the power and wisdom of God, and proclaim other ways to the Glory World? When will the day come that sinful men will recognize the fact that for thousands of years men have tried to deny the truth of the only way to the world of rest, but instead of establishing a way, they have, from first to last, failed completely!

Shall we ever see the day when sinners will realize and confess that the heaven is still open and the angels of God are still ascending and descending upon the Son of man? Shall we ever see the day when men universally shall recognize that heaven is waiting, that the way, Jesus Christ, is still the only way, the Royal Way, and that the fare is free to whosoever will? That would be a glorious day. That would come near being heaven on earth.

I see in some of your countenances this morning, marks of interrogation. Doubting Thomas said,

"How Can We Know the Way?"

I believe that he was honest and really did want to

know. He may have been a little fearful. He could not understand. Some of you are in a similar condition. You are honest; anxious for the truth; anxious to know the way, but you say that there are so many ways held out as being the only way, so many doctrines being taught, and how can we know the way?

I am just so firm a believer in God that I believe truly that if a sinner will honestly and sincerely come to the Lord in search for the way, that the Lord will show him the way, and lead him out, and if need be, will also send twelve legions of angels to direct him. God will not allow an honest seeker for the truth to go astray.

There are many tests which can be applied to convince any honest mind in this Christian land of ours of the true way. If you will honestly and prayerfully apply three tests which I shall mention, there can be no doubt, you will know the truth; you will know the way.

In the first place,

SATISFY YOURSELF AS TO WHETHER IT IS GOD'S PLAN

No matter what doctrine, what may be held out to you, your first duty is to search the Word of God. You are not justified in accepting any proposed doctrine or way, even though the Word says nothing against it directly. You need not accept one single plan unless you have a plain and undisputed, "Thus saith the Lord."

Men may try to explain away the testimony of the Lord, but that never changes the truth.

There are some things which are evidently wrong which God's Word says nothing about; but when it comes to the salvation of lost souls; when it comes to the way from earth to heaven, God's Word is plain. There is room for no possible shadow of doubt, and there is no reason why any soul should be in doubt. No man need despairingly cry out, "How can we know the way?"

The Word of God is a sure test. It will either prove or disprove any doctrine or way which may confront you. If you can find a plain sanction to the plan, you can make no mistake in accepting it. In fact you make a great blunder if you do not accept it.

While you turn to God's Word for evidence, just remember that you have the promise of the Holy Spirit to guide you into all truth. Commentators may help you. Men may help you, but the Spirit must and will reveal to you the secrets and the truth. Let the plain and unadulterated Word of God be your first test.

Second,

DOES THE PROPOSED PLAN CONTAIN THE DIVINE ELEMENT?

Is it of divine or human origin? We are living in a material world. We are moving toward a spirit world. We are at present bound up in humanity, in material. Somehow, somewhere, this corruption must put on incorruption. As living souls we must be connected with the spirit world. Spirit and material cannot be so thoroughly mixed as to become a single unit. For the soul, which is spirit, to enter the spirit world, it is absolutely necessary that there be a spiritual or divine avenue. Humanity in itself is void of the divine element and cannot possibly reach heaven through itself.

The way must be divine. God is divine. Jesus Christ, His Son, is divine. If mortal man ever reaches heaven, it is because he has gone over the divine way. It is utterly impossible for man to propose one single plan, knowing that he is void of the divine element, the main essential. Men may prepare successful ways from one city to another. They may go by land or sea because material man is dealing with material things. But man never can complete a successful way from a material world to a spiritual world. They cannot connect their souls with the divine through their own inventions, because man lacks the divine element.

It matters not what doctrine or what way may be thrown before you, or who may present to you a way from earth to heaven; it only requires a few moments to prove whether or not it contains the divine element. It may appear very reasonable to you; very convincing, but if you find it void of the divine element, you may rest assured that it is counterfeit, and you will do well to utterly reject it.

I find upon every United States silver certificate or bill, a peculiar net work composed of an endless line. When I find a bill with this line broken or blurred, I know that it is counterfeit. What is your hope, your belief this morning? Is it genuine, is it legal or is it a counterfeit?

The third test will invariably answer the question.

DOES THE PROPOSED WAY, OR THE WAY WHICH YOU ARE PURSUING, SATISFY THE HIGHEST DEMANDS OF YOUR SOUL AND CONSCIENCE?

Does your present course, your present belief and practice, actually satisfy you? Are you confident that there is nothing better? Are you sure that your present course is connected with God? Does the faith which you pretend to have make you a better man or woman at the present time? Does the way which you are taking satisfy you in regard to your past sin and mistakes? Are you sure that the Lord is satisfied, and that you are free from sin? Is the doctrine which you claim making you stronger spiritually? Is it giving you victory over temptation? Do you become better every day because of your present condition? Is it true that you are longing for something which you do not have? If you fail to become better every day, fail in temptation; if there is a longing for something better, it is evident that you are taking the wrong course.

Not only in the present, but will your course satisfy your soul when you are brought face to face with death? When your soul bids farewell to this world and takes its flight, will you then rest in ease? Will you be able to say that it is "well with my soul"? When you reflect over your past life, will there be dark spots? Will there appear sin which has not been repented of? Will you then confess that you have been pursuing a wrong course and that you have missed heaven at last? Today, if the death angel should knock at the door of your earthly tabernacle, could you open fearlessly, set your house in order and on your departure joyfully say, "I see the heavens open and the Son of man standing on the right hand of God"; and as you fall asleep in the arms of death, could you call upon God saying, "Lord Jesus, receive my spirit"? Or must you cry out, "Oh, my poor soul! what will become of you"? Will the way which you are taking satisfy you in the end?

Finally, when you stand before the great Judge of the quick and the dead, will the course which you now take satisfy Him? When your name is called and you must appear, will it be with fear? Will you tremble to stand before the all-knowing Judge? When the books are opened, and another book is opened, will you tremble wondering where your name will be found? Is there any doubt in your mind, whether or not your name is in the book of life? Is the highest demand of your soul and mind perfectly satisfied? You say, you are satisfied. The main question is this, Is the Judge satisfied?

If you will faithfully apply these plain, unquestionable tests, you shall know the way. If you can truly confess before God and man that the way which you are taking satisfies and makes you better daily; that it has taken away all past sins; that it keeps you from sin; that it will satisfy your soul at the death hour and that it will satisfy the great Judge, then you can make no mistake in continuing your course. But if you find that the opposite is true; that the way which you are pursuing is contrary to God's plan; that it is devoid of the divine element, and that it does not satisfy the highest demand of your mind and soul, either for the past, present or future, you can rest assured that you are taking a wrong course, and that it will pay you wonderfully to seek another.

We do confess that

THERE IS A WAY THAT SEEMETH RIGHT

unto a man, but the end thereof are the ways of death." It is a fact that people, who are apparently sincere, stumble and do not know the way. They hear so much and read and pray so little that they know not what way to take. The Lord has no chance to lead them. They listen to men who try nothing but to explain away the Bible; men who claim to be governed by reason and principle and not inspiration of the Scripture. They make Jesus Christ out simply a moral man and not a Redeemer. They are disgusted with the birth of such a Savior as Jesus Christ. They make Christ out an illegitimate child, and then blame the Christian and the Scripture for trying to cover the sin by blaming it upon the Holy Ghost. They have no use for the Word of God. They have no use for the Savior. All they claim is reason and principle. They are the characters known as infidels.

It will take but few words and glances at the three tests to see how disgracefully short

INFIDELITY

falls of reaching heaven. The infidel is of all men the most hopeless. Among them are found men of intelligence. They have their eyes open, but at the same time these same men are most hopelessly ignorant and blind. If there is such a thing as an owl-eyed fool, you will find it in the infidel. They are willfully ignorant, because they "Love darkness rather than light."

It is at once evident that infidelity has not one word of sanction from God's Word. The infidel falls down on the first test. God's Word is not back of him. He denies it from beginning to finish. God's plan is left entirely out and condemned as injustice, murder, immorality and falsehood, gotten up by some religious fakir.

The second test will inevitably condemn the whole theory of infidelity. It lacks the divine element, plain and simple, because it denies Jesus Christ. It denies His teaching, gives the God of the Bible no place. There is not one spark of divinity about the whole concern. The whole affair taken from the testimonies of the rankest infidels, is a human invention from start to finish. The whole affair is gotten up by men like Thomas Paine, Voltaire and Ingersoll. They admit of no divinity in the whole plan. They build upon their so-called ability to reason; upon their so-called principle. It is a deluded, hell-determined human affair from start to finish. The great essential, divinity, is left out. They try to connect themselves with God without a connection.

The last test cannot be questioned. Infidelity never did satisfy the highest demands of the soul. It never did make any one better in the present world. It is the very thing which brought France into her horrible Reign of Terror; into her immorality, licentiousness and her murder of hundreds and thousands of infants annually. It is infidelity that is sucking the life-blood out of France as a nation, and driving her to the back-grounds and finally to the darkest pit in hell. It is infidelity that has started America on the same track. Where is the man who dare say in the presence of a Mighty God that infidelity makes men and women better today? Ah, no, none dare say it! Infidelity is the key that unlocks the bottomless pit and turns the devil and his angels loose.

It takes a very ignorant or dishonest man to say that infidelity has done the world any good. Show me one institution of charity or learning which infidelity has established that did humanity any good; which has actually been a means of saving souls. You cannot find one.

Infidelity never did satisfy the dying hour. Tom Paine, the noted infidel, died drunk, cursing and swearing. His last words, "Stay with me, for God's sake, I cannot bear to be left alone; it is hell to be left alone," should be enough to satisfy any man of reason that infidelity is not the way to heaven. In his last moments he condemned his own book, "Age of Reason." When the leaders give up and condemn the way of infidelity, why do men blindly and foolishly follow after them?

Voltaire, another leader in infidelity, upon departing this life, left for us his dying testimony as follows: "I am abandoned of God and man; I shall die and go to hell."

Thomas Scott did not leave us without his testimony on atheism and infidelity. His last words were these: "Until this moment I thought there was neither a God nor a hell. Now I know and feel there are both, and I am doomed to perdition by the just judgment of the Almighty." Have you ever found a devoted follower of Christ who left such a hopeless testimony as these?

Do you need have me tell you whether these men realized the satisfaction of mind and soul both at the dying hour and at the judgment? Do you ask any more, "Is infidelity the way?" Jesus said, "I am the way."

Then I find a class who attempt to pave a way to heaven on their doubts. They are

THE SCEPTICS

They doubt Christ and His miracles. They doubt the conversion of Saul? They doubt the story of Jonah and the whale. They doubt the three Hebrew children in the furnace of fire. They doubt Daniel in the lions' den. They doubt Noah in the flood. They worry and fret about where Cain got his wife. The sceptic, "Just can't see where Cain ever got his wife." Just as though Cain had any less showing than himself. I would guarantee that if ninety-nine out of every hundred of you poor fretting sceptics had been placed in Cain's position you never would have found a wife at all; and if you had, you would have done worse than Cain. Cain was a man who had no time to worry about the other man's wife; he had all he could do to look after his own and that is what all you sceptics had better be doing. Why need you worry about Cain's wife?

How does the sceptic's way from earth to heaven measure up with the three tests? In the first place, he doubts God's Word from beginning to end. He builds upon his doubts, hence the divine element is lacking. His doubting makes neither himself nor any other man one whit better today, but makes hundreds worse. His doubts never satisfy at the dying hour; neither at the judgment. All of his doubts only make him miserable. They give him no promise of heaven. "Whosoever believeth in him shall not perish but have everlasting life." No promise for the sceptic, his way is without foundation, without satisfaction, without hope in the end. Jesus said, "I am the way."

THE UNIVERSALIST

is the most liberal yet of all. He says that all will finally be saved. All will be in heaven, none need suffer in hell. The Lord is too loving, too kind to punish any soul. He expects to get to heaven because the Lord is good. He expects to get to heaven and do just as he pleases in this world. He need not obey Christ. He need not deny himself from worldly desires.

One glance at the three tests will shatter the hope of the Universalist. God's Word says, that "He that hath the Son hath life, and he that hath not the Son hath not life." "The wicked shall be turned into hell and all the nations that forget God." "Not every one that saith unto me Lord, Lord, shall enter into the Kingdom of heaven, but he that doeth the will of

my Father which is in heaven." His plan fails on the
first test, because it is contrary to the plain Word of
God from beginning to end.

Under the second test there is nothing but human
opinion. There is no divinity there whatever. The
mind and sanction of Jesus Christ is not found there
at all. There is not even the least bit of good common
sense in it. It is a way set up by foolish men and the
devil. It is a Godless, Christless way to perdition.

And lastly Universalism does not satisfy the
highest demands of the soul and mind. It makes no
man better in the present world. The idea that men
shall be saved any way, regardless of their actions,
only tends to make men careless and wicked. Why
should a sinner repent and forsake his sin, if there is
salvation without? Why was Christ so foolish as to die
for sinners if there was salvation for us in our sin?
Universalism never satisfies the highest demands of
the soul. Makes no man better. It only increases
sin and wickedness. What a world this would be if
the doctrine of Universalism were universal! Men's
property, lives nor anything else would be safe. It
would be hell on earth.

The death hour comes stealing to the side of the
Universalist, and as he reflects over his past life, he
finds his sin still upon him. He has never been forgiven.
He has never been saved. But it is all too late now.
Before the judgment bar of God he must stand. The
great Judge has but one sentence, "Depart from me,
ye cursed, into everlasting fire prepared for the devil
and his angels." Oh, the dying testimonies which we

might give of the Universalist! They have all failed. But Jesus Christ who proclaimed that "I am the way" has never failed.

I shall not take the time to apply these tests to atheism, agnosticism, spiritualism, Dowieism, Christian Science, socialism and a catalogue of other "isms" that people are substituting for Jesus Christ and losing their souls by the millions. What I have said in regard to infidelity, scepticism and Universalism is also true of every other doctrine or faith which is not in harmony with Jesus Christ the Redeemer. Present whatever faith you will, and if it fails of these three tests, it can lead nowhere but to perdition.

It is very clear to the honest, sincere mind that

JESUS CHRIST

contains the divine element. He is according to God's plan and satisfies the demands of the mind and soul of men, both in the present and in the future. You may rest assured that if a man accepts Christ he will become a better man every day. He will be a blessing to his neighbors, and every one with whom he comes in contact. I need not argue with you this morning of the charitable institutions, the educational institutions, the world-wide institutions which have been established by Christian, believing people for the uplifting of humanity and for the saving of souls. If people will give Jesus Christ one half as much thought as they do their "isms" and unbelief, they would be fully convinced that Jesus is the way. But one glimpse of Christ, of His life, His work, His purity and perfection will convince any honest soul. The very fact that people refuse Christ shows clearly that they love darkness rather than light. They want a faith which does not require them to repent and forsake sin.

When we turn to the life and character of Jesus Christ we can readily see why He is the way. There is no doubt nor supposition about it. We can know

Why Jesus Christ is the Way

Come, let us reason together.

When God gave His law, He meant for man to obey it. He did not intend that man should break it. But contrary to God's intentions, men have voluntarily broken the whole law. What shall God do? Shall He change His laws? No, never. God's laws are immutable. That law must be kept. There is no hope without the keeping of the law. But men have all transgressed and broken the law. "All have sinned and come short of the glory of God." "There is not a just man on earth that doeth good and sinneth not." All men have failed save the Son of man, Jesus Christ. He Kept the Law Perfectly From First to Finish Not once was He guilty. Now the law has been obeyed for the first time. Now the law has been satisfied.

Do you see the secret of Christ being the way? Do you see the folly of men rising and proclaiming any other way than that of the Lord Jesus? Do you see the folly of Thomas Paine, Voltaire, Mahomet, Confucius, Joseph Smith, Dowie, Mrs. Eddy and such like? All are only men and women and all have broken God's law. How can they be the way? It is ridiculous for such people to arise with such proclamations, and it is most ridiculous and foolish for men and women to follow after and claim their faith.

For men to proclaim any other way save Jesus Christ would be equal to proclaiming that God has changed His law, which we know is an untruth. It is also equal to saying that there are other men who have kept God's law besides Jesus Christ, which we know also to be untruth. The fact is, we could not begin to name all the lies men must tell, and do tell, when they proclaim any other way to heaven except Christ. We cannot find a way in man. But when we turn to Jesus Christ, we have a far different picture.

I see in Jesus Christ

A Combination of God and Humanity

Christ did not change His divine nature to become a man; but He "took upon himself the form of sinful flesh." He sacrificed none of His divinity. He was simply clothed in human nature. He was simply a divine being dressed in humanity. You may dress an Englishman in a Chinese costume, but that does not make him a Chinaman. Christ took upon Himself the costume of humanity, but that did not change His divinity one particle.

At this point the infidel exposes his ignorance again. He stumbles and staggers and mocks at the idea of a divine conception of a man like Christ. He never stops to think that it never could have been

otherwise. Never could the Son of God have taken
upon Himself the form of man any other way. In
Jesus Christ there is a union of divine and human. It
required the work of one divine and human. His
divine nature came through the strength and work of
God and the Holy Ghost. His human nature was the
result of His human mother, Mary. It is a simple
problem when accepted as it really is.

Since Jesus Christ was wrapped up in the human,
it became necessary that He submit to the law of God
as well as other men. God had but one plan of salvation and that plan had been discarded by man. But
God establishes no new plan. The old plan must be
recognized, and since all men have gone so far away,
there is but one hope; we must have a substitute. We
cannot mend the law where we have broken it. All
we can do is to accept a substitute. God knew this,
and for that reason did not destroy His law but prepared a substitute, One who lived and obeyed the law
and gave offence in no single point. Now the law is
satisfied; it has been obeyed by One, and so far as
God is concerned, man is justified in accepting Jesus
Christ as his substitute.

Knowing this fact, it becomes very clear how it
was possible for Christ to fearlessly and with authority
proclaim Himself the only way. It also makes it clear
why no man will ever be able to proclaim himself or
his plans the way from earth to heaven. How foolish
for poor fallen man ever to think of preparing a different way from that of Jesus Christ! Or what is
more foolish is to see men leave God's plan and follow

some man-made machine. God's laws are still true and obligatory. Jesus has obeyed them all, and for this reason He may with authority proclaim to sinful men, "I am the way, the truth and the life; no man cometh unto the Father but by me."

I find in the Son of God another element necessary for salvation which cannot be found in any other. Since we have broken the law, and the law was not made void but established and must be kept, it becomes necessary that mercy and grace be administered. "The law was given by Moses, but

GRACE AND TRUTH

came by Jesus Christ." In Jesus Christ and in Him alone has man any hope of mercy and grace.

Because all men became sinners, condemnation is hanging over them. "The soul that sinneth, it shall die." What shall be done? Must all of God's human creation be eternally separated from Him? So says the penalty of the law. But thanks be to God, the law has been obeyed and the same hand which handed out the law has also handed out grace. It came through Jesus Christ. No man possessed it. It cannot be obtained from human hands. Grace is simply undeserved mercy, and man in himself does not possess that. We are all guilty sinners, and if our portion had been dealt out to us, we would all have died. But through the love of God, the mercy and long-suffering of Jesus Christ, grace has been handed out. The time was up for man to give an account, but through love and mercy, a few days of grace have been given us. The Lord still waits for sinners to repent and accept their substitute. Man has been robbing God, but Christ has paid the debt. Through grace we accept Him as our substitute. "I am the way."

Is it possible that men will wander here and there, and follow this man and that man, this "ism" and that "ism," this theory or that theory? Will men follow unbelief, infidelity, atheism and Universalism when there is not one spark of grace and mercy in them? Is it possible that sinners are so blinded that they cannot see that mercy and grace is the only thing that can spare them from the curse of a broken law? Can men believe for one moment that they can break God's law and then run away from it and find a way to eternal life without making amends or accepting a substitute where they have transgressed and failed? Refusing to listen to the condemnation of a broken law and seeking some other course will never do. The law still stands. The same law which condemns you will also save you. There is but one plan which has ever proved satisfactory, and that is God's plan. Repent and acknowledge your sin, accept grace and mercy; accept Jesus Christ as your substitute, as the One by whom we have grace and truth. "I am the way," because in Me there is mercy, grace and truth.

Before a telephone message can be sent from New York to San Francisco, it is necessary to first have a perfect connection from one city to the other. With proper connections, a conversation may take place as freely as at a distance of only a few miles.

Before an excursion train can run from Chicago to Denver, there must be a track laid which actually unites the two places. The same is true with the way to heaven. Before we can reach heaven there must be

A Perfect Connection

and this connection is found alone in Jesus Christ. He does actually connect the two places. His humanity and humility standing upon the earth and His divinity and exaltation reaching heaven. No man nor creature can claim the elements of Christ to the degree that in himself he is able to connect heaven and earth. Any man may reach part way. He can reach only to the extent of his humanity, but that comes far short of heaven. There must be a divinity and an exaltation to reach heaven.

I can now understand more fully why the blood of animals and why the works of men were not sufficient. I can see that in the blood of animals there was no divine element. It reached part way, but not to heaven. Faith in the coming Savior completed the connection under the law. I can understand more fully the cause of the wonderful birth and life of our Redeemer. I can now see the plan of God in not entrusting the work to man. There needs to be more to complete the connection. It required divinity. It is found in Jesus Christ.

No being can be found on record anywhere who can claim the origin, birth and life of Jesus Christ. He was in the beginning with the Father. He came to earth in a manner in which no other came. He lived a life which no other lived. He left the earth in a manner in which no other left it. No man was more severely tempted than He was. No man was able to sympathize with men more than He was. No man is free from sin, but He is. No man was so closely connected with God as He. No man connects earth and heaven, but Christ does. No man can proclaim to fallen men, "I am the way," but Christ can. He can, because He actually is the way.

When the heavens opened and the angels of God began to ascend and descend upon the Son of man, it was a testimony and a positive sign that the way from earth to heaven was now complete and ready to transport fallen men who were willing to repent and accept Jesus Christ. The great bridge which carries us across the eternal abyss is finished. It is an expensive bridge. It cost the life of the Son of God. It is still hanging between earth and heaven, not a dead but a living Savior. The way is still open; it is free. "I am the way."

Dare you ask again, "How can we know the way?" Can you say that there are so many prophets and teachers today that you cannot tell which is the true way? Do you dare to deviate from God's plan and accept man-made theories? Is the way not clear? Can you find another like the Son of man? Can you find one so human, so divine and so perfect? Can you find one with so much power and authority? Can you find one who has been tested and proven so often? Can you find a way over which the angels of God delight to pass? Can you for one moment doubt Jesus

Christ and trust the ways of men? Do you doubt Christ when He proclaims to fallen men that, "I am the way?" Do you believe it? Can you see how He connects earth and heaven? Do you see where man-made ways fail? Can you see where Tom Paine, Voltaire, Ingersoll, Dowie, etc., fail? Yet men will cling to these man-made schemes rather than to Jesus Christ.

But one conclusive reason why Jesus Christ is the way, is because,

IN HIM THERE IS PERFECTION

There is a satisfaction to the soul not found in any other. When I turn to His Sermon on the Mount, there are brought to my view teachings, both moral and spiritual, which can be found in no other. I find that the fundamental principle which our Savior taught was, "Be ye perfect." He gave His time, power and life to establish within us that teaching. It goes without saying that Jesus Christ could not give to us anything which He Himself did not have. He was perfect. He taught it. Nothing else but perfection would satisfy God.

Because He is perfect, I find in Him the element of love. "We love Him because He first loved us." Before sinful men had any desire to love the Son of God; before we were even willing to repent, He loved us. Though you may be a vile sinner today and feel that the Savior hates you, will you just remember that Jesus Christ loves you. No man can speak evil of Him, or nail Him to such a wicked cross but He loves them and prays to the Father to "Forgive them for they know not what they do."

Where is the man who can stand all manner of false accusation, all manner of ill treatment and still make no resistance? And if even a friend should step to his side and offer to protect him, could calmly say, "Put again thy sword into its place?" Could he willingly and lovingly forgive, though he had twelve legions of angels and could utterly destroy them?

Can you find an infidel, a sceptic, an atheist, a Universalist, a Dowieite, or any other unbeliever who would willingly, because he loves fallen men, go to the garden of Gethsemane, allow all the sin of the world to be placed upon him? Could he pray for them until drops of blood would fall from his forehead? Then lastly of all give himself up to wicked officers and be nailed to a cross? You at once say, no; man can do no such things. It requires love such as is found in none other than Jesus Christ. The way to heaven is by way of love. "God is love." Jesus Christ is love. He is the way. Will you simply believe and trust Him?

Perfection without peace of mind and soul is not a genuine perfection. Where is the soul that does not desire and long for peace? Men may apparently love confusion and disturbance, but that is not the highest demand of the soul. The Christless heathen goes daily to his idol for worship with hopes of finding satisfaction and rest of soul; but he returns and finds none. He is working through human inventions. In all heathen religions, men are trying to find God, but in the Christian religion God is trying to find men.

When men leave the altars of man-created worship, they leave with weary souls. The soul cannot be deceived. It knows a counterfeit. Peace cannot be found in human inventions. They may be as moral as they will; they may be as devoted as they will, but there still remains that desire for the divine. Men may lack in material things; they may even starve to death for want of natural food, but there is no suffering, no starving like that of the soul for the want of peace.

There is nothing which so much claims our sympathy as that of a wandering soul. One that is out on the raging sea of life where there is nothing but raging storms, wind and hail; a soul which is deluged in sin, looking for a haven of rest and finds none; a soul which is grasping at human-made harbors and finally without entering the haven of rest, it goes down without peace and without hope into a Christless grave.

If such is your condition this morning and you are sincerely and earnestly seeking rest and peace for your soul, we invite you to the One who said, "I am the way."

Because Jesus Christ is perfection, I find in Him also

Joy and Hope

None but those who experienced a walk on a prepared way can realize what it is. They alone can enjoy the peace of mind and soul. To know that sin is taken away; that the smiles of a loving Father are upon you;

that the glory world is for you, and that even now you are marching with the angels, is more than human tongue can express. Where is the religion, the proposed way from earth to heaven which contains joy and hope like that of the Christian. There is none. The way of the cross, the way of the One who said, "I am the way," is the only one which affords joy and hope.

Because He is perfect, I find in Him also

Eternal Life

I find that the character and elements of His way can be nothing but eternal life. As we climb day by day and year by year; as we reach higher levels of Christian experience, we pass over and use in our progress the elements or rounds found in I Cor. 13. Can there be a way more beautiful and more to be desired? A way of generosity, sacrifice, long-suffering, humility, charity, courtesy, temperance, honesty, patience, simplicity, knowledge, joy and hope? Do you wonder or doubt that angels ascend and descend upon such a way? Why do you hesitate to enter a road like this on your way to the spirit world?

While you reflect one moment, can you call to memory one single plan of salvation, equal in any degree to this one? No. I will confess for you, there is nothing equal to it. Will you then allow yourself to be deceived by man-made schemes, and refuse such an one as this? Do you not fear to arise and offer any more excuses? Do you dare to say that the way is so lonesome? Do you dare stand away and say that you are fearful and ashamed? Do you mistrust a way which the angels do not? Are you more than the angels? Are you satisfied to remain in your unbelief, your infidelity, your scepticism, atheism, agnosticism, immorality and sin of the deepest dye.

Within your soul you are repeating, "I know that Jesus Christ is the only way. I know it is God's plan. No man can prepare such a way. It is the purest, noblest way ever prepared. I know that if I take any other way I shall land in ruin. I know that the Lord's way will satisfy my hungry soul. I know it will satisfy its highest demands, and it will finally land me in heaven; but I will not come now. I will wait for a more convenient time."

Will you, my sinner friends, tell me what you gain by taking such a stand? When you know that Jesus Christ is the way; that He will satisfy your soul; that He will bear you across the river of eternal destruction and land you within those pearly gates? You must answer without mental reserve that you gain nothing, but on the other hand you are seriously losing. Think of it one moment, to become a Christian means losing nothing but gaining everything.

May I simply remind you as a closing thought that while the heaven is still open, and the angels of of God are still ascending and descending, it will not always be so. As the ladder of the patriarch stood for a time, then passed away, so the reality, Jesus Christ, will not always connect earth with heaven. "My spirit will not always strive with man." The way, Jesus Christ, will be taken down. There will be a great gulf fixed which no man can pass over. The Son of man will not always be our Mediator. He will not always be a Savior. The time is shortly coming when He shall be promoted from His present office to that of the Judge of the world. He will be no longer the "Royal Way."

Then you may cry loud and long as did the rich man, but all will be too late. The way is no more a way. The connection from sinful man to God is now eternally severed, never to be joined again. Will you come today and make Him your choice? Will you enter the "Royal Way" and continue until you reach the fair portals? Jesus is proclaiming, "I am the way." Will you send back the message with the angels, "Tell Jesus I'll be there?" My desire and prayer to God is that you may.

"Come for all things are now ready."—Christ.

"How shall we escape if we neglect so great salvation?"—Paul.

"Ho, every one that thirsteth, come ye to the waters, and he that hath no money; come ye, buy, and eat; yea come, buy wine and milk without money and without price."—Isaiah.

"One life; a little gleam of time between two eternities; no second chance for us forever more."

WHOSOEVER WILL

"Whosoever will, let him take the water of life free-ly."—Rev. 22:17.

I have just been thinking of a story which I read not long ago. A small boy who lived in Chicago had learned to trust Christ, he was away from his home, and out in a country town. He desired to go home, but had no money, no ticket and no friends. He asked God very earnestly that night for money enough to take him home. He believed that he would get it. Morning came but no money. He started for the depot, still trusting that the Lord would send him the money. It was nearing the time for the train to leave. One by one men and women were buying their tickets and yet he had no money. While the passengers were boarding the train he stood back without money and without a ticket. It looked very dsicouraging but the little fellow could not believe the Lord would forsake him. When all was ready and the passengers were on the train, the conductor called out, "All Aboard!" "All Aboard!" The little fellow said, "Why that means me too," and he board-ed the train without money and without a ticket.

But the conductor comes along collecting the tickets and the boy is compelled to confess that he has neither money nor a ticket. The conductor orders him to get off at the next stop and so he does. When all is ready again, the conductor calls out, "All Aboard!" and again the boy gets on. The second time the conductor orders him off and he obeys. Surely now there is no more hope, he thought. But to his surprise, he again hears the voice of the conductor, "All Aboard!" And again he boards the train. The conductor most severely began to rebuke him again. When the little fellow looks up with tears and says, "Well, conductor, you always say 'all aboard' and doesn't that mean me also?" When the conductor saw the sincerity and truthfulness of the boy's argument, he gave up and allowed him to ride home without money or a ticket.

Tonight the Gospel train stands at your door. Some of you are waiting for money, for friends, for feeling and everything but what you need. For nineteen centuries the conductor has been calling out, "Whosoever will," and yet people refuse the call. Remember the Gospel train makes but one trip and you need miss it only once to be eternally lost. When she pulls in at the Grand Union Depot of the New Jerusalem you will not be there, but you will hear your station called off at the lake of fire and brimstone.

I hope by His grace that I may make my final message so plain tonight that you cannot help but see with the boy, that surely the call includes you.

Will you go with me to the Isle of Patmos? There we see in that lonely place the exiled apostle. In front of him we see the rough, surging sea casting its foams high upon the rocks along the shore. Back of him are pillars of rock rising high above the sea. Not a single soul is there to share his lonely days. All is desolute and dreary.

We see him seated upon a rock with one hand on his brow and the other with a pen gliding back and forth over the parchment roll. The wonderful Revelation is being written. Warning after warning has already been handed out. Invitation after invitation has gone out to wandering souls. The exiled minister of God is ready to end his writing. He has come to the twenty-second chapter and the ninth verse, and is just in the act of sealing his work when the angel called a halt; "Seal not the sayings of the prophecy of this book."

Many have been the invitations to lost, wandering souls. But one clear, sweeping invitation must yet be given. Methinks I hear the voice say in quiet tones, "Let us be sure that all have been invited and that all will understand. Let us give no sinner one chance for doubt. Let us make it so plain that all will know that it is for them. Write the grand "Whosoever will." Make one sweeping invitation that no man can doubt.

Is it possible that you, my lost friends, can listen to such a voice and then say that God has never called you? Can you think of a word or expression which would more surely include you than "Whosoever will?" Yes; you say, that if he had written your name, John Jones or John Smith, or Mollie Brown, then you would be more positive that it meant you. But may I say to you that if your name had actually been placed upon the parchment roll in gilded letters bright and glowing as the midday sun, you would have no confidence in it whatever. You would have been sure to think, "Oh, that does not mean me; that is some other person; some other Jones, Smith, or Brown." The Lord knew how prone men are to doubt; so He wrote it in such a way that none would dare doubt. "Whosoever will" includes all.

I wonder tonight, if it were possible to get an inner view of Paradise whether the once exiled apostle would not be looking this way. Do his thoughts run to the lonely Isle of Patmos? Does he see himself once more as he is ready to seal the book and the angel calls a halt and says, "Before you seal it, make one final effort, give one final and universal invitation, make it plain; write the grand "Whosoever will?" I wonder if tonight he may be wondering whether sinners are accepting the invitation? Do you ever think that if there were such a thing as tears being shed in paradise it was because sinners refuse the invitation to come? Will you, wandering souls, in the presence of God and His final welcome again shut your eyes and say, "No; not tonight?" Can you, in the face of the eternal and incalculable price which has been paid for your soul, refuse to give it up to God and make those heavenly invitations and welcomes of none effect to you?

As I read the sacred volume from cover to cover, I find it filled with a continual flow of

Come! Come! Come!

The sum total of God's voice to men has been, COME. When I listen to the tender pleadings of the Spirit, I hear in loving tones the words, "Come home." When I listen to the pleading of the sinner's conscience, I hear it say, "Why do you not come home?" When I listen to the pleadings of the bride, the church, I hear the voice, "COME." When I listen to a loving mother's voice, I hear the tender words, "My son, my daughter, come home." Dear sinner, can you not hear a voice tonight calling you home? Do not deny it, do not quench the Spirit, but unlock and unbolt the door of your heart tonight and say to the voice, "Yes, I will come."

You say, "I want to come, and I shall come sometime, but

I Am Not Ready Tonight

I shall not accept, neither will I refuse it; I shall simply remain neutral." Listen, my dear friend, you know better than that. The Master says, "He that is not for me is against me." You cannot accept and refuse at the same time. You know that you cannot remain neutral. You know that in this matter you are either for or against Christ. You either stand by Him or reject Him.

You well remember how Pilate took the same stand which you now take. His problem was your problem. "What shall I do then with Jesus?" He realized that he had Christ on his hands, and that he must dispose of Him in some way, either defend Him or give Him over to the mob to be crucified. Pilate as well as you, knew that the man was innocent. He said, I will not defend Him, neither will I condemn him; I will remain neutral. He then turned and washed his guilty hands and said, "I am innocent."

I appeal to your own judgment, Was Pilate innocent? It was in his power to confess him, but because of his cowardly character, and for fear of losing his political position, just like men today, he refused and gave Him over to the crowd. No, never in this world was Pilate innocent! You know without the least argument that if ever man was guilty of the blood of Jesus Christ, it is the man who knew Jesus, who knew that He was innocent—who had power to protect and accept Him and still turned Him out to be crucified.

Will you listen one moment? It is a truth that there is not one single soul on earth, nor ever shall be, who has any more power and opportunity to accept and protect Jesus Christ than you have. You have no more trying problems than Pilate. You are not at the head of a nation. You must agree with me then, I repeat upon the authority of God's eternal truth, that you have Jesus Christ on your hands at this very moment, and, like Pilate, you must do something with Him. "Behold I stand at the door and knock." You must do one of two things; either you must let Him in or lock Him out. You must protect or condemn Him. There He stands innocently calling and knocking at the door of your heart, and if you refuse to hear, if you refuse to take Him and confess Him, you are just as guilty of the blood of Christ as Pilate or Judas ever was.

There can be no two ways about it; before you leave this building tonight, you will again either accept or reject the invitation. There are but two positions which can be taken. There is no middle ground. What will you do; accept Jesus Christ, your best friend, or will you reject Him? Will you calmly and without one mental reserve say, "Lord, what shall I do? Give to me the moral courage tonight to do what I know to be right." And when the Lord sends out the invitation to you again, will you send back the reply, "Yes, Lord, I have waited and rejected you long enough; I am not ready to come, but I will come."

There is another glaring fact connected with this matter.

Your Action on This Invitation Will Determine Your Eternal Future

Tonight you may forever seal your destiny. You may never meet the question again. When Pilate and Judas took their stand against Him, they determined forever their eternal future. Never again did they have such an opportunity to meet the question. Dear sinner, your experience can be no different.

There are but

Two Destinies

There is a place of eternal rest. Our Redeemer says, "I go to prepare a place for you." "And God shall wipe away all tears from their eyes, and there shall be no more death, neither sorrow nor crying, neither shall there be any more pain, for the former things have passed away." "And showed me that great city, the Holy Jerusalem . . . and had twelve gates and at the gates, twelve angels, . . . on the east three gates, on the north three gates, on the south three gates, and on the west three gates . . . and the city lieth four square; and the length is as large as the breadth, and he measured the city with the reed, twelve thousand furlongs . . . and the twelve gates were twelve pearls; every several gate was of one pearl; and the street of the city was pure gold, as it were transparent glass . . . and the city had no need of the sun . . . for there shall be no night there . . . and he shewed me a pure river of water of life, clear as crystal, proceeding out of the throne of God and of the Lamb . . . these sayings are faithful and true." This is one destiny; this is heaven. "And the Spirit and the bride say come . . . and WHOSO-EVER WILL, let him take the water of life freely."

There is a place of eternal punishment and un-rest. "And in hell he lifted up his eyes being in torment." "And the devil that deceived them was cast into the lake of brimstone where the beast and false prophets are and shall be tormented day and night forever and ever . . . and death and hell were cast into the lake of fire. This is the second death. And whosoever was not found written in the Book of Life was cast into the lake of fire." . . . But the fearful, the unbelieving and the abominable and mur-derers, and whoremongers and sorcerers, and idola-ters and ALL liars shall have their part in the lake which burneth with fire and brimstone. This is the second death." This is the other destiny; this is hell.

No other destinies can be found on record or in rational minds anywhere. Men and women are driven along as fast as the chariots of time can carry them to one of these two destinies. You may try to lock or turn the wheels, but you cannot. Which destiny do you choose? Will you accept the final invitation and start for heaven, or will you refuse and continue on your way to hell? Tonight you have your choice of the two destinies. After the grave you have no choice. Will you seal forever your destiny tonight? "Whosoever will, let him take the water of life freely."

You may be counting the cost of this final welcome. You may wonder what there is to be gained by coming. You may wonder what we are inviting you to. We cannot tell you all tonight nor in ten thousand years could we tell you all. But first of all we invite you to the Royal Way; not the ladder of the patriarch, but to the reality, Jesus Christ.

We invite you to

Jesus Christ

the One who said, "Come unto me, all ye that labor and are heavy laden, and I will give you rest." We invite you to the One who with authority and with power said, "I am the way." If you have been laboring under a hard master, and your work has been hard and unpleasant; if you have been disappointed in your wages, we invite you to Jesus Christ, whose yoke is easy and whose burden is light.

More than once have you confessed to yourself that the devil is a hard master. More than once have you threatened to quit him. More than once have you promised to try another master. Your work has been hard, miserable and unprofitable. But day after day you have refused; you have given Satan one opportunity after another to bind you closer and closer, until you have gotten to the place where you almost give up in despair. There is still hope for you, if you are willing to accept Jesus Christ, the only way; if you will accept the prepared way and climb round by round as the Lord gives you grace.

You may be heavy laden. Where is the sinner who is not burdened down and under a load which will sink him lower than the grave! Oh, that load of sin! It is driving thousands upon thousands to immature graves. But that is not the worst; it drives them to an endless hell. What a burden of soul! What a burden of heart! What a miserable life! What a wretched life! There is hope and relief for you, lost souls, if you will come to Christ. He has promised to deliver you and to bear your burdens. He invites you to come to the only way, the only hope.

But we invite you to more.

We Invite You to the Feast

spoken of by the prophet Isaiah. "Ho, every one that thirsteth, come ye to the waters, and he that hath no money; come ye, buy and eat; yea, come, buy wine and milk without money and without price." "Eat ye that which is good and let your soul satisfy itself in fatness." We invite you to a royal feast, a feast for your starving soul.

You go to the photograph gallery and have a likeness of your outward appearance taken. You congratulate yourself that you are so handsome. If God should turn on His powerful kodak and take the likeness of your soul and set it out before the public, I wonder whether you would congratulate yourself? Oh, if sinners could see their horrible-looking souls as God sees them, they would come to the feast. If it were possible for you to see that lean, hungry, starving skeleton of a soul of yours, you would repent. You would then know what the prophet means when he invites you to come and eat that which is good. He knows that you have been feeding your soul on trash, on filth and rottenness. He knows that your soul is lean, hungry and starving to death.

How many times have you actually seen yourself as you are? You were longing for spiritual food for your soul. You were longing for purer thoughts and purer words. You were longing to be pure in heart. You were really anxious for a changed life. You could see that death would be the final result of such a life as you are living. Your thirsty soul has already been calling for water; already the torments of hell have fastened their chains upon you. Already a death sweat is collected upon the brow of your soul. Relief must come soon, where can it be found?

We invite you to the feast. It costs you nothing, no money and no price. We invite you to the waters of eternal life, where your thirsty soul may drink and be satisfied. We invite you to the living bread, Jesus Christ, which came down from heaven where your soul may eat and delight itself in fatness. The call has gone out inviting sinners to come to the royal feast. Whosoever will, let him come. Will you come and satisfy that hungry soul of yours tonight?

What more can sinful man be invited to? Yes,

there is more.   Whosoever will, let him come to

PURITY AND HOLINESS

My Christian professing people, do you know what that means? I fear many of you do not. You have an idea that church-membership is all. Are you professing Christianity and at the same time living a filthy and immoral life? Are you still longing for those things which are impure and unholy? I must tell you upon the authority of God's Word that you are a disgrace to His cause and unless you repent you will be disappointed when you stand before the great Judge. I fear you will hear the verdict, "Depart from me, ye cursed, I never knew you." To be a child of God means to be pure and holy and free from the filth and bondage of immoral habits.

My sinner friends, we do not invite you to careless, inconsistent Christian professors. Keep your eyes away from such. Do not let them hinder you. You know that they are no model. We invite you to fix your eyes on Jesus Christ. We invite you to purity, and holiness, without which no man shall see God. We invite you to the highest, the noblest and the best, because it is for you. Would that I had words to express the beauty, the power and the glory of a strictly pure and holy life! Never until eternity shall we know fully the value and grandeur of it. We may know in part and we may enjoy it, but words fail to express.

You say that in your circumstances it is impossible for you to live pure and holy. You say that there is too much sin around you and there are too many temptations to sin. Listen one moment. Do you doubt God's power? The sweetest, purest, loveliest and most fragrant flower that grows springs up from the most filthy soil and water. No flower is equal to that of the water lily. No flower apparently has such unfavorable circumstances in which to grow. But when it is complete, it is the most noble and most handsome. Do not mistrust the power of God. "Consider the lilies of the field, how they grow." God is abundantly able to make and to keep you pure and holy in the most adverse circumstances. "Whosoever will, let him come."

When we invite you to purity and holiness,

WE INVITE YOU TO LIFE ETERNAL

"And this is life eternal that they might know thee the only true God, and Jesus Christ whom thou hast sent."

There is nothing which a man has that he deems more precious than his life. All that a man has he would give for his life. He would spend millions to extend his life for but twelve months, for six months, for one month, for one day. Nothing to man is so precious as his life. But with all this every man knows that death will come sooner or later regardless of his efforts, yet there is nothing so dear to him as a few moments of life.

When I turn from the physical life of man to the spiritual, I find a vast difference in the estimations which men put upon the two. Physical life to them is the all-important. Nothing is too precious but it is given to sustain the physical man; yet it is a sad fact that men will give away their eternal life, their eternal souls for less than nothing. Nothing is too worthless, but it may be had in preference to the soul, in preference to eternal life. Nothing can be so worthless, so filthy nor so damnable but man will give his soul for it. He puts no value whatever upon his eternal soul. He makes no provision whatever for the future world. Men are clamoring and struggling for life, and in the end have none. Then they wonder why and it is simply because they have a wrong conception of life. It is because they refuse Jesus Christ, the only real life. They refuse to believe that to know the only true God and Jesus Christ is eternal life. Life is more than they thought. They have clung to their physical life to the very last and now it must be given up, and they begin to look into the future world and see to their own eternal sorrow that life is gone, hope is gone, soul is gone and all is gone. "This is life eternal that they might know thee the only true God, and Jesus Christ whom thou hast sent." We invite you to life eternal. "Whosoever will, let him come."

I shall not attempt to explain fully that

WE INVITE YOU TO HEAVEN

We are unable to comprehend what it means. We have only a faint idea. The New Jerusalem, the Holy City—no night, no sorrow, no tears, no pain, no broken heart, no death, no temptation, no trials, no sin, nothing impure whatever. In the presence of God, of Jesus our Redeemer, the holy angels and our loved ones. There we shall be, not a few years, nor a few million years, but throughout eternity. There will be no end of peace and joy. The beautiful river of life will flow on throughout eternity. Sinners, all this is for you if you will accept it. It requires no financial capital. You may drink freely. "Whosoever will, let him take the water of life freely."

I hear the inquiring sinner ask, "Can it be possible that all this is free? Are there no conditions for me to meet?" Yes, there are conditions for you to meet. The main and only condition is that you be willing to accept the invitation. I have been thankful many times that the Lord never put such conditions to the invitation as men try to attach. Men make the way hard. They make it much more difficult than God has made it. Will you notice some of the conditions which men try to attach which God never requires?

Many sinners have I invited to come to Christ and almost as many have replied, "I know it is right, but

I DON'T FEEL LIKE IT"

They are waiting for a condition which is utterly impossible, and God knew that it was impossible. God knew that if He had given the invitation out that whosoever "feels like it," let him come, that there would not be one single sinner that could accept. Because the sinner never feels like it.

It just reminds me of the man who has been lost in the desert. He has no food. His physical strength is gone. He has no water. The hot sun, sand and wind have parched his lips, tongue and throat. A friend is passing by and sees him in this lamentable condition. He invites him to go with him to an oasis near by where water, food, shade and rest are plenty. The man raises his head from the burning sand and says, "Oh, yes, I do not doubt your word at all, but somehow I don't feel right, I do not feel like it." You at once say, "Foolish man, how can you feel right in such a condition? We do not expect you to feel like it. You cannot. You need not feel like it. Come anyway."

My sinner friends, it is even more so for you to say that you would like to come to Jesus Christ but you don't feel like it. We do not expect you to feel like it. God does not expect you to feel like it. He never asked you to feel like it. Talk about a man who is down in sin and transgressing the laws of God; starving his soul to death for the want of the Bread and Water of life, talk about such an one "feeling like it." Never. It is nothing but a trick of the devil to keep sinners away. I have never yet found a Christian who came to Christ because he felt like it. Sinners never did and never will. They must come regardless of their feelings. If you expect to wait until you feel like it, I must tell you honestly that you will never come. God knew what it meant when he said, "Whosoever will," instead of "whosoever feels like it."

I invite another sinner to come to Christ and he says, "I know I should, but

I Am Not Ready"

Well, thank the Lord, you are not required to be

ready. The Lord knew that men would not be ready. The Lord might have said, "Whosoever is ready let him come," but He knew that would cut out every sinner on earth, because no sinner is ready. They never have their affairs in the shape in which they want them.

The farmer says that he wants first to improve and pay for his farm, then he will be ready. But experience has proven, time and again, that the nearer he gets his farm paid the less he is ready to come to Christ, and nine cases out of ten, men who were almost persuaded when they were in debt with an unimproved farm were never touched or saved at all when out of debt and a well-improved farm.

The business man says that he cannot continue his business and be a Christian. He says he is not ready to come to Christ. They are not ready to lay down their business which is destroying their souls. The rich young man who came to Christ and lacked but one thing was not ready to follow Christ. Judas was not ready to follow his Lord honestly. Pilate was not ready to lay down his government position for the sake of Christ. Felix trembled but he was not ready. Thousands of similar circumstances may be mentioned. But let it be remembered that millions are being deceived and eternally losing their souls simply because they hold that they are not ready. The Lord never requires you to be ready to come to Christ.

How many sinners have told me that they will come when they get ready! Oh how foolish! Let

me tell you, my sinner friend, that you will not come
when you get ready, if such is ever the case. If the
time ever comes that you are ready, you will be sadly
disappointed to find that the Lord is not ready. Many
a man has cried out upon his death-bed for mercy but
found none. Apparently they were ready, but the
Lord was not. The Lord hardened Pharaoh's heart,
after he had hardened it five times himself, and he
might have been ever so ready to repent but God was
not willing. The Lord has made the conditions wonderfully easy. He never requires us to be ready; only
that we be willing.

Never have I found a Christian who accepted
Christ because he was ready. Man never is ready and
if he ever comes to Christ he does it against his own
carnal will and at a time when least ready. "Whosoever is ready?" No. "Whosoever will."

I ask a third sinner to accept Jesus Christ and
he confesses that it would be right but he

Don't Want To Just Now

He wants to wait until he "wants to." He is being
deceived. He has an idea that he must want to come.
The devil has blindfolded him. The devil and modern secret societies work together in their initiation.
They both must blindfold their applicants. They are
not allowed to know what is being done around them.
If the devil can keep a man out of heaven on the point
that he thinks that he must "want to come" before he
can come, he has nobly accomplished his purpose.

The Lord knew that carnal man never did, nor
ever would want to come to Him. He never de-

manded that we "want to." He makes the invitation so simple and so universal that no man and no condition is left out. The sinner need not even want to come, thank the Lord, but he may come any way if he will. "Whosoever will may come." Whosoever is ready has no promise. It is a matter of will and not of desire.

But I meet another class of sinners who do not accept Jesus Christ because they say, "I would like to but

I Am Not Good Enough

I am too sinful. The Lord does not want me." They think they must be good enough, or the Lord will not receive them. Why will people allow themselves to be deceived? "This is a faithful saying and worthy of all acceptation, that Christ Jesus came into the world to save sinners." Why do men prefer to believe the devil rather than God? The Lord never demands that sinners be good enough.

We cannot deny the fact that many of the popular churches today have reached the point where a sinner must be about so good, apparently, in dress or society, to say nothing about his filthy soul and heart, before they will receive him. If they are good enough in money, in the social circle and fashionable adornments, they are received; if not they are rejected, and looked upon with scorn and contempt.

But the Lord makes no such demands. He never requires so much money, so high a standing in society, nor does He require you to be "good enough," as you call it. It matters not how poor you are, how

low-lifed and low down in sin you are; how miserable
a wretch you may be, you are still good enough to
come to Christ. The Lord does not demand of you
to clean up before you come. He wants you just as
you are. You cannot make yourself one whit better.
Every move man makes alone is downward. It takes
the Lord to elevate.

There is no praise, there is no invitation to those
who are "good enough," but every promise in God's
Word, every invitation in God's Word is for "whosoever will." You say that the conditions are hard.
Can you think of one point which would have made
them easier to be accepted? Every effort man makes,
every suggestion man offers, makes it more difficult.
Think for one moment; the promise of eternal life
and of heaven is not for those who "feel like it," not
to those who are "ready," not to those who "want
to" and not to those who are "good enough," but for

Whosoever Will

It is a matter of will and not feeling and emotion.
It is a matter of will and not being ready. It is a
matter of will and not a matter of wanting to or
being good enough. It is a matter of will and not
intellect. All that the Lord requires of you is that
you be willing to believe in Jesus Christ; that you
have faith in God. You say you cannot believe.
Where is your will power? You cannot believe that
two plus two equals five because that is a self-evident
falsehood. With all your will power you could not
believe it. When you heard of the San Francisco dis-
aster, you did not hesitate one moment to believe it.

You believed it, not because you were there and saw it, nor because some one told you who did see it, but you believed it when you heard of it and read of it, because you were willing to believe it. You gained the consent of your will to believe, and so it must be in believing in Jesus Christ. All that the Lord requires is that you exercise the will power which He has given you. The promise is to those who will believe. Whosoever will believe in Jesus Christ may come.

You say you would like to repent, but you do not feel like it, you are not ready and you cannot. You have no promise on such conditions. You know and confess that our Savior spoke the truth when He said, "Except ye repent ye shall all likewise perish." But you say, "How can I? I would like to, I want to." That is not the question, dear sinner, the Lord does not demand of you to want to or to like to; all that He demands is that you exercise your will power and become willing to repent, regardless of your "want to's" and "like to's." The invitation goes out to whosoever WILL repent.

The sinner says, "I want to come, but I must leave my friends. I want to come but I am not ready just now. I expect to come sometime." The truth is he prefers anything else rather than to come to Christ. He is making the conditions much harder than God has made them. If God had made the way half so hard as you are making it, there would not be one single sinner saved. And that is not all, you have no promise whatever of eternal life while you cluster around you such hard conditions.

The Lord does not demand that you "want to come." He does not demand that you "expect to come." All that He asks of you is that you be "willing" to come. The question is, Are you WILLING to come to the "Royal Way?" Are you WILLING to come to the feast? Are you WILLING to believe in Jesus Christ? Are you WILLING to repent? Are you WILLING to be justified, converted, regenerated, sanctified and receive Christian graces? Are you WILLING to climb the ladder? All of this is not fancy, it is actual, it is real. "If ye be willing and obedient, ye shall eat the good of the land; but if ye refuse and rebel, ye shall be devoured with the sword; for the mouth of the Lord hath spoken it."—Isaiah.

It is free, it is ready and it is for you. There is no excuse for one single soul to stay away. No man can be so poor nor so destitute but that he may come. No man is so rich that he can buy himself out of hell. The water of life is free, and more than that, it is ready this very moment. You need not wait until you reach the glory world to receive it; but this very night it is ready and you may have it. But the best and most glorious of all is, that it is for every sinner. It is for you and no other being in heaven or hell. Jesus Christ died for you. He arose again and ascended into heaven for you. God sends out His final invitation for you. All of this is for you, all is ready, all is free to "whosoever will."

Can you resist longer? Can we make the invitation any clearer? Can you listen night after night to the voice of God inviting you home and not come?

Will you continue in your course until like Pharaoh, your heart will become hardened like a stone?

It Is God That Calls You

He has no pleasure in your downward course. He has no pleasure in the death of the wicked. He has no pleasure in seeing you suffer daily from your sin. He wants you to be present at the marriage of the Lamb. He wants you to be present at the royal feast. He wants you in heaven throughout eternity. Because of His longing desire for the welfare of your soul, He is sending out the call to you, through His Word, through His Spirit, through His Gospel ministers, through the prayers of His faithful followers. Can you resist Him longer? All this time you have been refusing God, refusing His invitation. Will you not once and forever give up and say, "Here, Lord, am I, I give up all I have, I will accept the invitation."

I Hear the Savior Calling

"Come unto me." "Sinner, come home." How often have you heard the voice? How often have you refused? Have you caused sadness in the heart of your Savior by going astray and refusing His call? Are you one of the lost sheep which He is seeking now? Can it be possible that tonight again, while you hear the tender pleadings of a loving Redeemer, while you are so near the kingdom, while you are upon the very threshold, that you will turn a deaf ear and a cold shoulder to Jesus Christ?

Had you not better come to your Savior and acknowledge that you have shamefully treated Him and beg His forgiveness? Had you not better come and believe in Him and make Him your Savior? Would it not do your soul good to know that tonight as you retire that you can lay your head upon your pillow and slumber, knowing that the smiles of a loving Savior are upon you? Would it not be a satisfaction to your soul to know that you could claim the Lord as your Shepherd? Would it not be a satisfaction for you to know that you have done what you could? Will you refuse and turn away from your door the best friend this world has for you?

The day upon which Henry's father was laid into the cemetery was drawing to a close. In the evening at the supper hour mother prepares a lunch, and the brothers and sisters are gathered around the table at their regular places. Mother says that she will not sit down because she is not hungry. Father's place is vacant. They all hesitate to eat. Mother is crying. One after the other, the brothers and sisters begin to cry and leave the table. The evening passes slowly along until bed-time when one by one they begin to retire. Father always locked the door before he went to bed. But tonight father is not there. Henry, being the oldest, must perform that duty. He walks up to the door and turns the lock but the awful thought strikes him, "Tonight, this awful dark night, I have locked my father out." Sinner, that is what you are doing every night that you refuse to let the Savior in. You are turning a lock on your best friend. While Jesus is knocking at the door of your heart, will you not let Him in?

But I hear another voice tonight.

A Call from the Celestial World

The voice is announcing the birth of a Savior which is Christ the Lord. It is the voice of angels. I cannot but believe that the angels are calling. They desire to have sinners come home. There is joy among them over one sinner that repenteth. If there is joy there, I have reason to believe that they are interested. Why should they not be interested when they are ascending and descending upon the way? Can you refuse the voice and pleadings of the angels? If there is such a thing as tears being shed in heaven, I believe it must be among the angels when they behold the love of Christ, the invitations going out to sinful men, and they see sinners, who know the truth, who hear the pleadings, and instead of coming home they refuse every call, every pleading and every invitation. It seems to me if anything would cause the angels to weep, that would. Wandering souls, will you come home tonight? Will you send a message to Christ with the angels telling Him that you are coming?

But I must speak of other voices. I wonder tonight if it were possible to get a glimpse and

A Voice from Paradise

whether there would not be invitation after invitation coming from loved ones who have gone before. Do you remember that father, that saintly mother, that brother, that sister, that son, that daughter, that child or that friend who was dear to you? Do you remember their last words? Did they invite you to come? Did they invite you to meet them in heaven? Did you promise them that you would? What preparations have you made? Do you wonder whether they know your condition? Do they know that you have broken your promises? Yes, I have all reasons to believe that it is possible for them to know. We shall be no less wise over there than we are here. I have reasons to believe that in the spirit world the soul is developing continually and is gaining more wisdom continually. I believe, while we have no means of communication as some would have it, that the souls of loved ones do know infinitely more than we in our humanity. And I have no reasons in the least to doubt that those gone before do know, in part at least, what your condition is. I have no reasons to doubt, if we were able to behold them, that there would be invitation after invitation coming this way. We might be able to see that brother, that sister, looking this way and wondering if brother or sister will start for heaven tonight. We might see that little child looking this way wondering if papa or mamma is coming tonight. We might see mother anxiously looking this way wondering if her son or daughter will come tonight.

I have known sons and daughters who could stand at the bed-side of a dying mother, they could stand by and see her lowered into the grave and never shed a tear. I have witnessed those sons and daughters melt to tears and confess Christ later when the words and memories of mother came back to them.

When the pleadings of mother were again heard, they came forward and gave themselves up to Christ. Thank God for every saintly mother. What cannot be accomplished by her life may be by her death. "It is not all of life to live, neither all of death to die." Work many times only begins after the death of some loved one.

There was a man whose little boy died. The father seemed very strong and bore the trial apparently easy. But after the funeral was over and the boy had been laid away in the grave, the father walked out into the front yard and there in the corner he saw a small wagon and a little spade. Beside the wagon were little foot-prints left behind by the feet that were gone. But now the man who appeared strong, when he saw this, wept aloud, wept like only a child could. Did he hear that little voice?

There came a gentle knock at the door of a German poet. When the door was opened a sweet-faced child walked in with a bunch of beautiful violets. She handed them to the poet saying, "This is a gift from my mother." "Your mother," said the poet, "why she is dead." "Yes," said the child, "that is true, but you remember when she died I asked you to write a verse for her tomb and you so kindly did so and these are the first violets that have bloomed on mother's grave. I have gathered them and like to think that she sends them to you with greetings." It was more than the poet could stand. Only a flow of tears could relieve him.

Have you noticed those flowers on some loved

one's grave? Do they not speak to you louder than
any human voice? Do they not call you up higher?
Do they not make you anxious to cross over and be
with the departed ones? Do you not desire to see
God, to see Jesus and the angels? Will you tonight,
while the heaven is still open, and the angels of God
are still ascending and descending on the Son of man,
lift up your voice with the poet,

> "I have wandered far away from God,
>   Now I'm coming home;
> The paths of sin too long I've trod,
>   Lord, I'm coming home.
>
> "I've wasted many lonely years,
>   Now I'm coming home;
> I now repent with bitter tears,
>   Lord, I'm coming home.
>
> "I'm tired of sin, and straying, Lord,
>   Now I'm coming home;
> I'll trust thy love, believe thy word,
>   Lord, I'm coming home."

Not until then will you be set free from sin, and
enjoy the present life. Not until then can you expect
to meet those loved ones over yonder. Not until then
dare you expect to be like Him and to see Him as
He is. It is only then that you become one of the
"whosoever will." Only then can you sing with a
pure and free spirit,

> "No more I fear the longest night,
>   Nor dread the darkest day;
> For one is always near my side,
>   Along the homeward way."

THE END